TOURISTS CAN SAY THE DARNDEST THINGS!

TOURISTS CAN SAY THE DARNDEST THINGS!

Exploring Historic Charleston, South Carolina

To: Jackie
Best Wishes!
Al Miller
June 25, 2022

AL MILLER

Editorial Director,
Alada Muima Shinault-Small, MA, CIG

Copyright © 2017 by Al Miller

ISBN: 978-0-692-03352-4

Library of Congress Control Number: 2017902343

"Charleston Old and New" c by John W. Jones, Artist; Author of the book & exhibition, Confederate Currency: The Color of Money, Images of Slavery in Confederate and Southern States Currency and Beyond, www.colorsofmoney.com

All photos were taken by Al Miller and A.M. Shinault-Small unless otherwise indicated.

Images courtesy of Pixabay are found on pp. 49, 59, 60, 68, 79, 108 & 125.

All Rights Reserved. No part of this book may be reproduced or transmitted in any form or by any means, electronic or mechanical, including photocopying, recording, or by any information storage and retrieval system without written permission from the author, except for the inclusion of brief quotations in a review.

Printed in the United States of America.

This book is dedicated to my Mother, Dorothy Mae Leonard Miller; and siblings: Mary Lee Miller McFarland, James Miller, Jr., Dorothy Ann Miller, Purvis Miller, Sr., Bernard Miller, Johnny Lee Miller, Sr., and Jenevie Miller Rowell.

This book is also dedicated to my nieces, nephews, aunts, uncles, and other extended family and supporting friends.

This book is dedicated to my high school classmate and friend Martin Lane (known as Marty).

This book is dedicated in memory of my loved ones:

James B. Miller, Sr., Father; Doretha Robinson Davis, Grandmother; Willie McKinley Miller, brother (known as Will); Pauline Deloris Miller Green, sister; Catherine Deloris Miller Williams, aunt (known as Aunt Sister); Elizabeth Parsley, aunt; Purvis Miller, Jr., nephew (known as P.J.); Darian Miller, nephew; Rev. Daniel L. Simmons, Sr., dedicated cousin and confidante (known in the family as Dan); Rev. Clementa C. Pinckney, cousin, friend and Fraternity Brother; and Rev. Levern Stevenson and his wife, Maxine Ruff Stevenson, cousins.

I dedicate this book to Lillie Bell Singleton Smith and in memory of her husband Richard N. Smith, Jr.

This book is dedicated in memory of the victims of the Mother Emanuel AME Church tragedy on Wednesday, June 17, 2015. Mother Emanuel 9 victims were Mrs. Cynthia Graham Hurd, Mrs. Susie J. Jackson, Mrs. Ethel Lance, Rev. DePayne Middleton-Doctor, Rev. Clementa C. Pinckney, Mr. Tywanza Sanders, Rev. Daniel Lee Simmons, Sr., Rev. Sharonda Coleman-Singleton, and Mrs. Myra Singleton Quarles Thompson.

This book is dedicated in honor of the survivors of the Mother Emanuel AME Church tragedy: Mrs. Jennifer Pinckney, Mrs. Felicia Sanders, Mrs. Polly Sheppard and two children.

Lastly, this book is dedicated in honor of Mother Emanuel's congregation, its family members and friends, and all others who were impacted by this deep tragedy.

Acknowledgements

First and foremost, I thank Almighty God, The Creator, for giving me strength and knowledge. I thank my parents Dorothy Mae Leonard Miller and the late James B. Miller, Sr. for my existence; being born the seventh of ten children. Thanks to extended family members and friends who are too numerous to name for your love and support.

I thank my cousin Bruce Levern Stevenson for being a "listening ear" many late nights while truck driving and I read excerpts from the book.

Thanks to local Charlestonians for sharing your stories and insight which have afforded me a unique perspective and a better understanding of Charleston's history given that I'm a "cumya" and you are "binyas".

Thanks to Edna Wright Taylor and her daughter Jonzetta Taylor Goodwin for use of family photos and information. I wish you and your family continued prosperity vending in The City Market. You are truly a piece of Charleston's history.

Thanks to visitors who have taken my guided tours and attended my lectures. Thanks for your many referrals. Your kind and thoughtful deeds are numerous. Your presence and comments are most appreciative and assisted in making this book possible.

Thank you Charleston for your deep, rich history. Visitors flock here from around the globe to take in all that you have to offer.

Thank you to the many enslaved Africans, and those who preceded you, for your contributions that made Charleston and the surrounding areas what they are today. You cannot speak, but I and other guides speak for you.

Thanks to my friend Audrey F. Partlow whose comments about a Charleston tour guide in 1986 inspired me to become one.

Thank you DeEthel H. Brown, my friend and confidante, for your undying love and support. You know I love you, too.

Thanks to Chuma Nwokike and Chuma Gullah Gallery for carrying the works of artists John W. Jones, Jonathan Green and others which depict Lowcountry scenes and Gullah Geechee Culture.

Thanks to Artist John W. Jones for your permission to use your marvelous painting for the book's cover. Thank you for your creative artwork and I wish you continued success.

Special thanks to Dr. June P. Murray for your insight and your dedication to proofreading this book.

And lastly, heartfelt thanks to Alada M. Shinault-Small, Director of Operations, Sites and Insights Tours, for your hard work, love, grace and dedicated service in publishing this book. You have truly made it happen. I could not have done it without you. I love you much.

Table of Contents

Introduction		**xi**
1	**Dull Moments? Not Here!**	**1**
	Tourists Can Say The Darndest Things!	*9*
2	**Emanuel African Methodist Episcopal Church**	**11**
	Emanuel AME Church c.1910	*15*
3	**The Emanuel 9: On Losing Two Relatives**	**17**
	Conversation with Daniel L. Simmons, Jr.	*28*
	Photo Montage: Looking Back In Retrospect	*42*
4	**Gullah + Geechee = Gullah Geechee**	**47**
	Tourists Can Say The Darndest Things!	*52*
5	**Da Burra aka The Borough aka Ansonborough**	**53**
	I Remember	*60*
6	**The Market**	**61**
	Charleston Eagles	*68*
7	**Yep, We Have A French Quarter Too!**	**69**
	The Great Earthquake of 1886	*79*
8	**Broad Street, South Of Broad & The Battery**	**81**
	Slave Auctions Historical Marker Unveiling	*98*

9	**The Holy City: Churches, Churches & More Churches!**	**99**
	Tourists Can Say The Darndest Things!	*108*
10	**The Eastside**	**109**
	A Tribute to the Late Mr. Philip Simmons	*121*
11	**Until The Next Time….**	**123**
	Color The Hat Man!	*125*
Bibliography		**127**

Introduction

My South Carolina high school history course at Rains-Centenary High, Rains, South Carolina, afforded me a keen appreciation of the state's history. Most of the focus was on Charleston, the oldest city in the state, credited for the state's humblest beginnings. My first trip to the old city was in August 1968, I was age 12. My father, James B. Miller, Sr., was hospitalized at the Medical College of South Carolina (now the Medical University of South Carolina) with a bad case of pneumonia. In addition to visiting my father, crossing the Cooper River Bridge was one of the highlights of the two-hour trip from Marion County. That bridge was replaced in 2005 with the Arthur Ravenel, Jr. Bridge. My brother Willie (Will), age 15 at the time, had visited my father the previous Saturday and spoke highly of the tall, narrow bridge. "It's scary! It goes high into the sky and you can see it from a distance before crossing it," he said with excitement. During this period our family traveled very little and taking advantage of any trip of any reasonable distance was exciting. Prior to this trip, traveling to Florence (approximately 30 miles from home) and Atlantic Beach (approximately 50 miles from home) were the occasional extent of our out-of-town travels. On small trips and for shopping in downtown Marion and Mullins, SC, my family of 10 children plus my parents caused a very tight squeeze in my father's Plymouth station wagon, and later Buick station wagon.

Other recollections of my first trip to the old city were experiencing the Charleston single homes along Meeting and Calhoun Streets, and my first elevator ride at the hospital to my father's room on the 6th floor. The style of the Charleston single houses was different. There appeared to have been hundreds of them as we ventured to the hospital! I later learned upon becoming a tour guide that these homes, long on the side and narrow to the front with the porches facing either to the south or west side, were originally built this way to catch the southwest breezes.

My second trip to Charleston was in 1973 during my senior year in high school. My Journalism teacher, Mr. Thomas Smyth, Jr., two other students and me attended a Journalism seminar one Saturday morning at Baptist College at Charleston (now Charleston Southern University). As a high school student, I had the determination and desire to attend college. Mills, factories and tobacco farms were plentiful in Marion County and nearby Horry County during this period. As for me, those occupations were not career choices. Every summer from age six up to this point, working on tobacco farms was inevitable. Most workers referred to the occupation as "working in tobacco". The older I became, the more I disliked tobacco, even though eventually machines had replaced much of the manual labor. I'm grateful for the experience though; it taught me the necessity of work.

My third trip to the historic Charleston area was when I stepped onto the campus of Baptist College in the fall of 1974 as a freshman. The counsel and encouragement of high school teachers, family members and Mr. Wesley, my Guidance Counselor, made that a reality.

Earning a Bachelor's Degree in three years with a double major, English and Speech/Dramatic Arts, I graduated in the spring of 1977. My parents didn't earn a lot of money; and I knew if I didn't apply myself in college, I most likely would have returned to Marion Co. seeking employment in those unwanted jobs. My mother, Dorothy Mae Leonard Miller (whom I will call Mrs. Dorothy Mae) did not play; she would have seen to it that I seek some kind of employment. Grants, loans, employment off campus and work study programs (including being a reporter for the college's newspaper *The Buc'n Print*) were my tools of survival while in college.

After graduation, I returned to Marion Co. briefly to seek summer employment. Future plans were to attend the University of South Carolina's Graduate School of Journalism in Columbia, SC in the fall. My summer employment search for a clerical or administrative position wasn't successful; therefore, I returned to Charleston to job hunt. So at this point, graduate school followed by a Journalism career had to be placed on the back burner – survival was my immediate concern.

Eventually, I was hired by Sears, Roebuck and Company in Northwoods Mall, North Charleston, in the Credit Department as a Credit Counselor. At this point, I had no idea that this job was the beginning of my work career in Charleston. Then on December 12, 1977, I was hired by Sea-Land Service, Inc., the largest containerized steamship company in the world at the time, as an Export Documentation Clerk. My employment with Sea-Land lasted 22 years and 4 months with clerical positions mainly in Cargo Claims and Customer Service, and these unionized clerical positions paid above-average wages.

Life is so full of uncertainties and who can predict where the direction of a conversation will end? Although my passion for history was evident, especially

Charleston's, little would I know that in the fall of 1986 (now residing in the Charleston area 12 years) that I would be interested in becoming a Licensed Tour Guide by the City of Charleston. A friend and Charlestonian Audrey F. Partlow and I conversed during this period regarding Charleston's history and about a local licensed guide that she knew. Because of that conversation, my affection for Charleston's history and the impact of tourism on the local economy inspired my interest in pursuing a career in tourism.

In order to become a Licensed Guide, the City administered an oral and written exam with the bulk of the information deriving from their publication *The Guide Notes of Charleston, South Carolina*. The latest edition was published in 2011, *The City of Charleston Tour Guide Training Manual*. My career as a Licensed Tour Guide commenced in 1987 after passing the exam, and I mainly conducted private and step-on tours (the guide steps on board a chartered bus or a van and conducts the tour) while maintaining my full time Sea-Land job as well. Later, I was employed a few months on weekends by American Sightseeing and afterwards briefly as a Guide at Drayton Hall Museum Plantation. Desiring to be my own boss, my company, Sites and Insights Tours, Inc. became a reality in 1993 after purchasing my first tour vehicle, a 15-passenger van. I provided tours on a part-time basis during the week after my Sea-Land job and full time on weekends. Conducting tours on chartered buses, vans and walking tours continued.

A. P. Moller-Maersk Line purchased Sea-Land on December 11, 1999 and the company became Maersk Sea-Land. All union clerks and some managers and supervisors were laid off. My last day was April 14, 2000. This change afforded me the opportunity to operate my tour business full time and to pursue a career in real estate. Then I bought a mini bus in 2003.

This book will focus on many of my experiences as a tour guide over the last 30 years with emphasis on what people have said and done on my tours. In the 1990s, I started paying serious attention to the hilarious comments that folks made and decided in 2001 to write a book about it. Comments and reactions to various sites and attractions, shared stories, jokes told, responses to each other and to happenings outside of the tour bus along with lots of information and photos on Charleston history and culture are all included for your reading pleasure. Some of the names used are fictitious, but the remarks and stories are not. In addition, I agreed with my editor that sharing all of the collected material in one book would result in a very huge volume; therefore, two sequels are currently in progress. This edition covers a hefty portion of touring around downtown Charleston. Book Two will include touring the rest of downtown and throughout James and Johns Islands, and Book Three will highlight adventures while touring other nearby areas.

Finally, I continue to partake of the water (it's said that you can't leave Charleston once you drink the water) and the scrumptious Low Country cuisine that has kept me attracted to this gloriously historic and culturally-rich area for the last 4 decades. However, although I consider myself to be a Charlestonian by now, I'm often reminded by the locals that I'm a "cumya", a Gullah expression meaning that I wasn't born here, but I came here. Someone native to the area is called a "binya", s/he has been here. Charleston, however, is like many American cities – you can live there 1,000 years, but if you weren't born there, you'll always be considered as an outsider.

TOURISTS CAN SAY THE DARNDEST THINGS!

1 | Dull Moments? Not Here!

Dull moments are few on tours. There are agreements, disagreements, some like the truth, some don't, there's a gripe every now and then, and people will be people. Often, Heaven only knows what folks glimpse outside of the tour bus and how they process it. It could be a bumper sticker that reads, "Ex-wife in trunk," or "Ex Mother-in-law in trunk." Or, it could be a petite woman in tight jeans standing on a street corner waiting for the traffic light to change, prompting Barbara Smith from New York City to interrupt the tour suddenly by announcing, "Those jeans are so tight, I'm sure she used Crisco oil to get into them!" On any tour there's laughter, fun and we all learn at the same time. Mr. Tour Guide, as I call myself, loves people and enjoys what he does. Touring is my fun job, and I've been accused of being "a mess," "an instigator," "funny," "something else," "mischievous," "a teacher," and more - but it is all good. So Reader, let's take a Sites and Insights Tour, laugh, have fun and learn.

"Hello! My name is Al Miller, owner of Sites and Insights Tours. Welcome to Charleston." And from 2004 to the present, a typical greeting by me, Mr. Tour Guide, might go this way with my speaking in the Gullah language: "Way unna chillun from?" (Where are you from?) Visitors' responses range from smiles and laughs to excitement and confusion. I've heard "What did you say?" "What?" "Whoa!" or "You went foreign on us for a moment!" Those who understand the language have stated, "That's Gullah you're speaking," or "That's Geechee you're speaking." We'll talk more about Gullah and Geechee in Chapter Four.

It's a good gesture to find out where everyone's from. Here's a typical example of what goes on during introductions. Starting with the couple seated up front to my right, the woman says, "We are the Weavers - Patricia and John from Ft. Smith, AR. We're visiting Charleston for the first time, and we're looking forward to the tour." Then the man from the couple to my left speaks, "We're the

Hagoods from New York City. This is our second visit to Charleston and our first tour. My Grandfather came to NY from Charleston and we're here searching our family roots." Next, the lady seated behind the Weavers says, "My name is Phyllis Hawkins from Silver Spring, MD, a suburb of Washington, DC. My husband is here for a conference and I decided to take a tour." Next, the lady behind the Hagoods says, "Hello, my name is Regina Alexander Whitman from Knoxville, TN. My husband could not make the tour; he's playing golf with his buddies." And the lady next to Ms. Whitman says, "Hi, my name is Helene Mead from Fairview, TX. Regina and I have been friends since childhood, we were in each other's wedding, and my husband Frank is playing golf with her husband Jim. We decided to let the men do their thing and we women'll shop and tour and spend their money." Everybody laughs. The next person announces, "My name is Dewayne of Virginia Beach, VA. Following Dewayne, a woman from Durham, NC says, "I'm Elizabeth Beasley and as for this man seated next to me, I don't know who the hell he is and where he's from." "This man" was her husband Larry, and he laughed. Lastly, the spokeswoman for the crew seated at the back of the bus says, "My name is Susan. We are the Mullin family of Jefferson City, MO. This is my husband Phil, my mother-in-law Edith, my son Jeffrey and his wife Connie, and my precious grandchildren Michael and Ashley." Michael, who appears to be around six years old, prefers to speak for himself as opposed to being represented by his grandmother. He raises his hand and remarks, "You didn't ask me where I was from." So the lad introduces himself, and everybody applaused his bravery.

On numerous occasions I've been asked by visitors, "And where are *you* from?" Some African Americans who're familiar with Gullah have told Mr. Tour Guide that he doesn't sound like he's from Charleston. Occasionally, then I'll give a quick response in Gullah like: "And how unna know I ain from ya?" (How do you know that I'm not from here?) With that response some think Mr. Tour Guide is a Charlestonian. Then I'll reveal the truth – "I'm not a Charlestonian. I'm originally from Mullins, SC, a small town in Marion County, 116 miles north of Charleston between Florence and Myrtle Beach, about a two-hour drive from Charleston. I came to Charleston in the 1970s to attend Baptist College which is now Charleston Southern University in North Charleston. After graduation, Charleston became home, and the rest is history. I've been a tour guide since 1987." I've chuckled to myself often through the years that Mr. Tour Guide drank the water and ate the fish, so now he's hooked and cannot leave.

The Charleston Visitor Reception and Transportation Center (VRTC), pictured right, is located at 375 Meeting St. and

is the starting point for most tours. Bordered by John St. to the south and Ann St. to the north, the City of Charleston moved the Center to its present location in May 1991. This larger building and grounds afforded more space to accommodate visitors, local tour buses and chartered buses, provide adequate parking, house a gift shop, offer two sets of rest rooms and more. It was built in 1856 by the South Carolina Rail Road as a freight depot. Similar buildings nearby on John and Ann Sts. in the former suburb of Wraggborough were also freight depots and passenger stations of the South Carolina Rail Road (S.C.R.R.) William Aiken, Sr. (1779 – 1831), president of the company and father of Governor William Aiken, Jr. (1806 – 1887), resided nearby at 456 King Street at the corner of Ann St. The building was also company headquarters.

An iron gate known as "The Welcome Gate" sits in front of the VRTC on the Ann St. side across from the front entrance. The late Mr. Philip Simmons, a renowned blacksmith from nearby Daniel Island, Dan's Island as he called it, was commissioned by the City to create it, and it was placed in this location in the early 1990s to welcome all visitors into Charleston. Flags of the nation, state and city are stationed near it. Simmons became a wheelwright at first, following his apprenticeship at age thirteen under Calhoun St. blacksmith Peter Simmons, no relation. In 1938, he transitioned to ornamental ironwork and then made his first gate in 1944. Later, this master craftsman trained a nephew and cousin. His works can be seen throughout the Charleston area, at the South Carolina State Museum in Columbia, at the Charleston International Airport, and at two sites at the Smithsonian Institute in Washington, DC., to name a few. Mr. Simmons celebrated his ninety-seventh birthday on Tuesday, June 9, 2009, and he died just less than three weeks later on Monday, June 22nd. "Is that the man on the film inside the Visitor Center?" visitors ask. Remembrances come to mind from those who had the honor of meeting him and visiting his blacksmith shop at 30 ½ Blake Street. "He was a wonderful, nice man," "I'm glad I had the privilege of meeting him at his shop," and "We didn't know he passed away," are some of the comments made often. You'll read some more on Mr. Simmons in Chapter Nine.

The prior Visitor Information Center at 85 Calhoun St. was substantially smaller than the present VRTC. During my early tenure as a tour guide, most motorized tours departed from the Arch Building, as it was called because of the wide arched passage through the first

"The Welcome Gate", crafted by master blacksmith Philip Simmons & located near the Charleston Visitor Reception & Transportation Center entrance.

floor. Constructed around 1800 and rebuilt in the early 1850s, it's located in the former suburb of Ansonborough. Tradition says that it was built for wagon trade and had a wagon yard behind it; wagons loaded and unloaded passengers under the archway. It's the only original building remaining between Anson and Alexander Sts. It was spared during the clearing of a number of structures in that African American section of the neighborhood, known locally as "Da Burra", to make way for construction of the Gaillard Municipal Auditorium in the late 1960s. The Auditorium was recently rebuilt, and it re-opened in 2015 as The Charleston Gaillard Center. Meanwhile, the arch was enclosed at some point through the years, and the building now houses the City of Charleston's Civic Design Center. Read more on Da Burra in Chapter Five.

Tradition also says that the Arch Building became a whore house for Whites after the Civil War in 1865 and a whore house for Blacks in the 1940s. In the 1970s it became the Charleston Visitor Information Center. "Still accepting visitors," many have uttered. "What a history this building has; if only the walls could talk!" is hardly an understated remark. Imparting the history of 85 Calhoun St. almost always sparks some excitement, and the brunt of the laughter and amazement has been discovering the building's various uses. During tour pick-ups there, after presenting the whore house history, many tour guides have been known to say to their guests with a straight face, "And it is still accepting visitors." To my knowledge, no guides have ever lost a few teeth or knocked to the ground by tourists thinking that that comment insinuates that they're being compared to whore house clients.

The former Charleston Visitor Information Center at 85 Calhoun St.

The round earth quake bolts or rods that are visible on the Arch Building were implanted between the ceilings after the Great Earthquake on August 31, 1886 (more on the earthquake later). As a result, in the event of future quakes, the building will be much more stable. A female reporter from Los Angeles, CA, thought of the activity that may have taken place in the building, especially during the great quake, and jokingly commented, "I'm sure lots of shaking occurred in that building!" Sharing the reporter's "innocent" remarks on numerous tours have prompted many to say, "I expected a man to say that and not a woman," and "Some women talk and think as dirty as men." In November 2007, an older gentleman from a Road Scholar group summed it up this way with no shame, "In other words, that is where you got screwed. Now that's a good one for your book, Mr. Miller!"

Since most people yearn for the true history of Charleston no matter how it sounds, many prefer hearing the words "whore house" as opposed to "House of Prostitution". Despite whatever term is used, it means the same. Elliott Moore of Wayne, NJ said, "Besides, it was a meeting place or visitors center for a different reason before it became the center for Charleston's tourists and visitors." Mr. Tour Guide takes it as a joke when the question arises, "Where are the whore houses today?" Inquiring minds sure do want to know. And depending on the mood of the tour, some ex-military men who were once stationed in Charleston (especially the Navy when its base was open) remembered this kind of activity occurring near the Base on "The Strip" along Spruill and Reynolds Avenues in North Charleston. And as for others, this kind of activity occurred in many cities (even today), and after all, it's the oldest profession in the world. According to locals, there were many whore houses throughout the Charleston area. History is history, and it is much appreciated by the tourists.

After much discussion, using the term "House of Ill Repute" is appreciated by some adults when children are on board. On the other hand, depending on the ages of children, some adults prefer using the word "whore" because children need to know and understand the truth since "whore", or a variation of it, is heard in the media and in recorded music often. This leads to an incident in 2003: after a boy around age six from TX heard the words "whore house", he asked his mother, "Mama, what's a whore house?" She said to him, "Mr. Miller brought it up, and he'll explain it to you." Then I began to give hard thought to how I was going to explain this to a young boy. That word was never mentioned again on that tour, and apparently the lad forgot about it. There are always lessons to be learned, and that particular lesson for me was: Be careful what you say in the presence of children; when you think that they aren't paying attention, they really are and will question what is said, especially when a new word is spoken and curiosity kicks in.

Back to the subject of 85 Calhoun St., tours are challenging with some church groups in giving the history of that building. In the late 1990s, while conducting a tour on a 47-passenger chartered bus for a Black Baptist church group from Augusta, GA, the Minister posed the question about the whore house. "Now Mr. Miller, what did they do in places like that?" I replied, "Reverend, if I didn't have all these church folks on this bus, I would certainly tell you." Sharing this story to others through the years, many women have replied something like, "The nerve of him to ask such a question, as if he did not know, playing innocent. I'm sure he's been in some of those places himself." By this time, the tour usually heats up on the subject, and Mr. Tour Guide transforms into Mr. Instigator: "Rumors have it that some of the Black preachers have been known to frequent some of those houses in the city." This remark raises many eyebrows, especially among the women, who often shout out shockingly, "Black preachers?" And my response would be, if my maternal grandmother, Doretha Robinson Davis of Marion, SC, were on this tour, she would say, "Darling, he's a man isn't he?" I continue to share with my guests what she would have said about preachers in whore houses. My grandmother passed away in 2001, I surely miss her kind and gentle spirit.

In June 2006, my mother, Mrs. Dorothy Mae, was successful in fulfilling my request to locate an old chamber pot or pee pot (as I called it growing up). These pots were salvation to thousands who didn't have the privilege of an indoor bathroom. "Thank God for indoor plumbing today!" said a woman from NH. Mrs. Dorothy Mae purchased it for $20 at a store in Marion, SC that carries old merchandise. These pots are a rarity nowadays, and I pleaded with her that no matter what one costs, buy it. Storing the pot at the front of the tour bus has become an added addition and a reminder of my childhood and others', as well as a lesson for those who never had the experience of using one. Also, the pot comes in very handy as a tip jar. "Is that pot what I think it is, Mr. Miller, for the bathroom?" someone asked innocently one day while boarding the bus. Someone else said, "Look at that chamber pot, that's history. You are bringing back a lot of history. A historical pot sits on a historical tour!"

Years before the pot was a part of the tour, I made a restroom stop and a female voice said, "If you would have had a necessary on this tour bus, this stop would not be necessary." So, since the summer of 2006, my tour introduction has been something like this while holding up the pot and making eye contact with everyone: "This is an historical tour, therefore, there will be no restroom stops. This is the restroom. You may go to the back of the bus or you may use this cubby hole behind the driver's seat. The user will have the job of dumping it and not the tour guide." Most adults know what the pot is, so there's lots of laughter. Someone said once, "Because you're writing a book about your tour guide experiences, if you make no restroom stops, then a few paragraphs may be written about *you!*" Of course, Mr. Tour Guide assures his guests that there will be bathroom stops - but in the event of an emergency, we do have a backup. I have yet to drum up enough courage, however, to take the pot when touring on board chartered buses with large groups.

The majority of younger folks have no clue of the pot's use and think it was used for cooking. In the fall of 2006, a little boy from NC who appeared to be around 6 years of age kept his eyes on the pot as I swung it from left to right. He appeared to have been hypnotized. Being curious about his response, I said to him, "Young man, do you have any idea what this is?" With an innocent and sincere voice, he responded, "A crock pot." At that moment, I said to myself, "Poor little kid, if he only knew the story of this pot." Sharing this incident has become a laughing moment. Marvin Kent, a middle-aged man from San Francisco, CA later said, "Yes, a crock pot but only for a different kind of stew." In March 2011, Ellen said, "And a different kind of crock." In the latter part of 2008, a lad commented that the pot was used to hang by the chimney to collect ashes. And another lad said, "That pot is used to heat water on the stove."

African Americans generally refer to the pot as "the pee pot", "the chamber pot", "the slop jar", "the pee can" and "the piss pot" and Whites have called it "the honey bucket", "the honey pot", "the thunder jug", "the chamber pot" and "the potty". Folks from the United Kingdom with their unique accents have called it "the po" and "the guzender", meaning that it goes under the bed. A young twin from GA said, "I guess it was called the thunder jug when you had to do No. 2." Folks from parts of the Caribbean have called it a "chimmy".

Historically, sophisticated Charleston Whites called the pot "the necessary" and it sounds much more proper to say, "Bring me the necessary." Ralph, a New Yorker, said, "Because it *was* necessary!" A necessary was a piece of fine furniture, often mahogany, in which the seat was a lid. Upon raising the seat, the pot was visible underneath it. Basically, it was an elegant way to handle one's business.

Many have confessed that they haven't seen a pot like this in years, and how well they remember using it and/or having had the task of taking it out to empty and clean. "My grandmother kept the night pot by her bed, and I had to carry it out the next morning," said Abigail Creighton of Dayton, OH. Some comments have been about grandparents who had indoor plumbing but kept the pot

Mr. Tour Guide & the pot.

by the bed at night to eliminate walking to the bathroom. Mary of OH said, "My grandmother stayed with us, and my father used to get so angry because she kept the chamber pot by the bed and the bathroom was a short distance away." Theresa of OK said, "Al, my grandmother told me and my siblings to bring her the shit pot." Old school domestic workers (including many grandmothers) referred to it as just that - the shit pot. Some of these remarks are rather unpleasant to some listeners, but most agree "it was what it was."

In 2004, Mrs. Davis from Wilmington, NC was a part of a senior citizens group, and she gave her opinion on historical sites as she witnessed them. She appeared to be full of wisdom, and I found her remarks to be quite fascinating. She knew the pot as a slop jar and quickly said in what she thought was a whisper, "Lord, we had to carry that shit out." I was speechless and amused, and I laughed aloud along with others who had heard her. Suddenly realizing that she was louder than she intended, Mrs. Davis quickly placed her right hand over her mouth and looked embarrassed. I told her not to feel embarrassed. She had had a flashback of when she and other Black women who labored as maids and housekeepers for Whites had the regular task of carrying out the pot, emptying and cleaning it.

TOURISTS CAN SAY THE DARNDEST THINGS!

"Could I buy a home with a student loan?" asked a college student.

Around 2001, I took reservations from a woman from Asheville, NC who was residing at a local hotel. Feeling comfortable with her over the telephone and knowing that Asheville was in the Blue Ridge Mountains, I said, "I see that you're a mountain woman." And she said, "Yes, and I brought with me my mountain man."

On the Old German Fire Company at 8 Chalmers Street:
"Did the Germans put the fire out with beer?"

While on the Eastside in August 2012, we saw a lady wearing a short red dress. I said, "Look everybody at the woman with that short dress on, she is really wearing it!" An older lady at the back of the bus said, "And I guarantee you, if she were to reach over and pick up something, she would give you her full name and address." Now that's a comment that I hadn't heard since I was a child.

A gentleman from New England asked,
"Can you buy these old homes with Confederate money?"

2 | Emanuel AME Church

EMANUEL AME CHURCH, 110 CALHOUN STREET, WAS FOUNDED IN 1818. IT'S THE oldest Black congregation in Charleston and the oldest AME Church south of MD. The Reverend Morris Brown, who later became the second Bishop of the AME Church, spearheaded bringing the AME movement to Charleston which had become official in Philadelphia, PA in 1816. The Reverend Brown was a free

Black Charlestonian and a shoemaker who resided on Anson at Wentworth Streets. He also owned rental property at 94 Smith Street. Both Morris Brown College, Atlanta, GA and Morris Brown AME Church, Charleston, were named after him.

Many of Charleston's Black Methodists, enslaved and free, had become discontented with Bethel Methodist Church on Calhoun and Pitt Streets and eventually withdrew over burial disputes. Under the Rev. Morris Brown's guidance, three churches emerged named the Bethel Circuit - one in Ansonborough, one in Hampstead and one in the French Quarter.

Denmark Vesey, whose birth name was believed to have been Telemaque, was a member of the Hampstead church. He won $1500 in the East Bay St. lottery in 1799 with which he purchased his freedom for $600 from Capt. Joseph Vesey who enslaved him and opened a carpentry business. His attempts to free all of the enslaved people in the area on July 14, 1822 failed when William Paul, an enslaved laborer who was privy to the plan, mentioned it to another enslaved man, Peter Desverneys. Desverneys was troubled by this news and sought advice from William Penceel, a free Black tinplate worker. Penceel's advice? Desverneys should most definitely tell his owner. The owner was out of town, so Desverneys told his mistress instead about Vesey's freedom plan. As a result, the authorities were notified when Desverney's owner John Prioleau returned, names of Vesey's helpers were identified as various Black men were interrogated and imprisoned and Charleston soon became abuzz with talk of a planned rebellion. As a result of all of the obtained condemning info, the Hampstead church was destroyed by arson and the other two Bethel Circuit churches were forcibly closed. Furthermore, Denmark Vesey and five others were hung on Tuesday, July 2, 1822 between 6-8 am in the Blake Lands, which was an area north of Line St.

In case you've wondered what happened to those who initiated the thunderous avalanche that blanketed Charleston for years to come: William Penceel, the "advisor", got $1000 and an exemption from the free Black tax. Peter Desverneys, who he advised to reveal Vesey's plan, became a free man, received a $50 annuity and an engraved silver pitcher. Further, he eventually amassed considerable wealth, to include hefty real estate in Wraggborough, and he owned enslaved Blacks. William Paul, the enslaved laborer who initially told the plan to Desverneys, was banished from the US. Further, Whites became extremely fearful of more uprisings, and uneasy about the roles that free Blacks (like Vesey) could possibly play in them. So, the General Assembly passed acts to tighten control of free Blacks in 1822. For example, all free Black or biracial males (labeled mulattoes and mestizos then) ages 16 and up had to be placed under the care of a guardian. The guardian was required to be White and respectable. In 1823, an act was passed that prohibited the return of any free Black citizen who left SC. We'll be talking more about Denmark Vesey in Book Two.

Meanwhile, the Bethel Circuit members continued worshipping, but secretly, now that they no longer had houses of worship. They re-emerged after the

Civil War, consolidated the three congregations, officially instituted their church and then named it Emanuel, meaning "God with us". Then they purchased the Calhoun St. land, but sadly, their first church on that site, an 1872 wooden structure, was destroyed during the August 31, 1886 "Great Earthquake".

The present brick Gothic Revival edifice that's elegantly trimmed with marble was built in 1891. Known as "Mother Emanuel", the sanctuary retains its original floor, pews, pulpit and communion rail. The original gas light fixtures remain mounted near the electric ones. The pipe organ was installed in 1908, and it still plays very richly.

The Rev. L. Ruffin Nichols was Emanuel's pastor when the present church was built. He and his wife Anna are entombed in the basement below the steeple. When the church underwent a major renovation in the late 1940s to include being stuccoed, the congregation thought that it would be appropriate to bring the remains of the Nicholses from the church's cemetery to the church. Numerous Blacks who are members of the African Methodist Episcopal Church or those familiar with AME Church history find it satisfying to know that The Rev. & Mrs. L. Ruffin Nichols were the parents of retired AME Bishop Decatur Ward Nichols who passed away in 2005 at the age of 104 in Huntington Station, Long Island, NY.

When touring the basement to see the tomb of the Rev. and Mrs. L.R. Nichols, more older adults prefer not viewing the tomb than children and young adults.

Some act as if the dead would suddenly come alive and overtake them, and others see it as strange and eccentric for the dead to be buried inside the church. I remind visitors that this European tradition is not uncommon for the clergy and members of their families to be entombed inside the church structure. Most young brave souls are not frightened in the least by the tomb experience. Their curious minds find it intriguing; and if they had their way, they would open the tomb and examine the remains. On the other hand, some young and old visitors see it as a frightening experience and stay away from the tomb. Some of the elderly find it difficult to go up and down the steep steps leading to and from the basement. The most common questions and comments by children are: "Can you see them?", "Are they dead?", "What happens if they wake up?", "I'm scared!", "Are they both in there?" Some of the brave boys go, "I'm not scared, I wanna see 'em!" If they would awaken, I would most likely outrun the children. "Those bones will not hurt you; do not worry about the dead but the living," is often stated. And another popular question once the tomb is viewed that always brings laughter to those with dirty minds is when the innocent children have asked, "Who's on the top, him or her?"

On Saturday, April 18, 2009 as the history of Emanuel was being imparted, a bride and groom were seen exiting the church. Mr. Tour Guide tooted the tour bus horn at the couple, and waves were exchanged from the couple to the bus. A brief discussion was exchanged as if this were the same bride seen earlier departing the Mills House Hotel. The men thought that they had the right bride until one of the women said, "That's a different girl, the gown is different and she is slightly larger than the bride at the hotel." The discussion quickly ended, and the tour continued. Fellas, you have to admit – overall women just tend to be more detail-oriented.

Above - The rear of Emanuel AME Church as seen from the parking lot.

Tourists Can Say the Darndest Things!

Mother Emanuel AME Church, photographed about 1910: The 1891 brick Gothic Revival- style structure is embellished with marble. After a late 1940s renovation, the church was stuccoed. The front stairway and the two windows above the doors were refashioned also, and notice the brick-paved Calhoun St. The late Rev. Clementa Pinckney initiated a fundraising campaign in 2014 to construct an elevator on the east side of the church. The elevator was dedicated in June 2016.

Photo from the Margaretta Childs Archives at Historic Charleston Foundation

3 | The Emanuel 9: On Losing Two Relatives

Wednesday, June 17, 2015 left a long stinging scratch on many hearts, still with no scab....

Entering through this door:

11 adults + 1 child = 1 dozen assembled to read the Word, discuss and learn.

1 adult aiming to relax & wait in her life partner's office + 1 of the 2 children - patient like Job, anticipating family time after a very l-o-n-g day.

1 whose name and image would dominate the media for what seems like forever.

Exiting from this door:

8 saints who were rolled out, forced abruptly to leave all who they knew + 1 who tried to stay, but joined them too.

2 adults + 1 child who walked out, never to be the same - ever ever again.

1 adult + 1 of the 2 children who walked out as well, no more family time to have as they knew it - ever ever again.

1 who slithered out, metal life-taker in hand, casually driving away into a Holy City's summer night - the welcomed guest: hate-filled, guilt-free, proud, and for sure - stark raving mad.

– A.M. Shinault-Small

REFLECTIONS: *EXCERPTS FROM A CONVERSATION WITH DR. JUNE P. MURRAY AT AL MILLER'S HOME, SUNDAY, FEB. 19, 2017*

On the Rev. Daniel Simmons:

Dan and my father were first cousins. I've known Dan since my childhood. His father and my grandmother were brother and sister. His father, Uncle Moses Simmons (known as Uncle Mose), connected our family's leg with other family legs of the Miller-Simmons family. And in that regard, Dan followed in his father's footsteps. He was born in Mullins, SC which is in Marion County, the same county in which I was born. He and I became close when he lived in Columbia, and when he moved to Charleston in 1999 we became very, very close. I really miss Dan. We spoke just about every day, sometimes twice a day. He was retired and we depended on each other. Dan gave sound advice, and he was a good confidante. He was a friend, a teacher, and was like a big brother. What I miss the most is the fact that I don't get to talk to him anymore, see him, see him passing by the house in his car and tooting the horn (we lived in the same subdivision). I don't get to see him at The Battery while I'm touring (many times he would be sitting out there, especially after his retirement), or see him some Sundays while I'm touring by Emanuel Church and I would see him leaving, and he would blow his horn. It's strange going to his house and he's not there.

When his car was released from the church after the shooting, his gun was found on the seat. Had he taken the gun into the church that night, I know we would have a different story. We think that Dan was trying to get to his car to get his gun (after Dylann Roof starting shooting) to shoot Roof, but that didn't happen....

Dan touched the lives of so many people, especially after he retired. When we arrived at Greater St. Luke AME Church for Dan's funeral, I had never experienced such support from people. It was hot that day, it was h-o-t! And people had been standing out in the sun for a while holding up handwritten posters stating such nice expressions of sympathy and support. And that's what amazed me — people being out there for so long. There was lots of donated bottled water. It really did something to me because here was somebody's funeral that I was really close to.

I thought the funeral was very dignified, just like Dan would have wanted it. The final funeral for him in Columbia at Bethel AME Church was crowded, but not like it was here in Charleston. I gave remarks at both funerals.

Dan would be proud to know that I joined Ebenezer AME Church. I had been visiting for a while and joined six months after he died. Attending Bible Study has strengthened me, enlightened me and helped in this grieving process.

About that day, June 17, 2015:

That day was a typical summer day. I had conducted two tours. Dan and I didn't speak that morning, for whatever reason. I arrived home about 5:00 PM and the phone rings. It was Dan and he said, 'I'm on my way to Bible Study, talk to you later,' something of the sort. The conversation was very short. A typical summer day like that (June 17) — I might return a few calls, watch television, type letters, and eat. Next thing, I'm dozing in the chair. Well about 10:00 PM, I was awakened by a phone call from a college friend Rev. Lavern Witherspoon who asked, 'Have you heard of anything that had gone on tonight at Emanuel Church?' I said, 'No.' He continued, 'because I've received several phone calls from persons who are not from Charleston about a shooting at the church.'

My first thought of a shooting was perhaps in the church's parking lot or somewhere other than inside the church. We hung up and I began to make calls. I turned on the television and there was the news about the shooting, and that it had affected the Bible Study Class. My home phone and cell started ringing. Also, when I first heard the news I didn't think about Dan because 10:00 PM at night he would have been home from Bible Study which usually started at 7:00 PM, but later learned that there was a meeting before the Study and it started at 8:00 PM. Then I immediately called Dan's cell and home a number of times, but was unable to reach him. Now I'm really getting worried and it's about 10:30 PM and I called Dan's son Deon – Daniel Simmons, Jr. – but the family calls him Deon. I said, 'Deon, turn on the television, there's been a shooting at Emanuel Church that has affected the Bible Study Class, and I know your Dad went because he called and told me where he was going.' We were on the phone a while. Before hanging up, Deon said that he has to come to Charleston tonight, he was going to relax a little bit more and would get on the road (from VA).

Upon arrival to Charleston Deon said he would come directly to my house because I had a key to Dan's house.

I later received the news from Deon while talking back and forth while on the road early the next morning that Dan had passed away on the operating table at the Medical University of SC Hospital, according to the coroner. Deon had actually seen that night on television the EMS unit bringing Dan out of the church on a stretcher. One of our other cousins, Ernest Miller of Brooklyn, NY, saw it on television too.

Dan was the only one of the nine victims who didn't die at the church. That night, the phones kept ringing, ringing, ringing. I couldn't hang up for two minutes before it started again. Everybody was saying what they heard. By this time it was about 11:30 PM and it was announced that Clementa Pinckney was dead. I think I got to bed around 2:00 AM and couldn't sleep. So I got up, started crying, and read some Scriptures which calmed me. Then I was able to return to bed and got some sleep until Deon arrived around 7:00 AM Thursday morning. We embraced and went directly to Dan's house.

On the morning of June 18, the shooting at Emanuel Church dominated the news all over the world. I later learned that day that there were nine victims. In addition to Dan and Clementa, I knew three of the other victims: Mrs. Susie Jackson, Mrs. Ethel Lance, and Mrs. Myra Thompson.

The next few days were trying times. I had tours scheduled, and every tour included the history of Mother Emanuel Church. Phone calls, texts and emails were overwhelming about this tragedy from numerous persons who had taken the tour expressing their condolences and prayers, and remembering the history of the church.

This is the cover of Dan's funeral program.

The Order of Service
Celebrating the Life
of
The Reverend Daniel Lee Simmons, Sr.
Tuesday, June 30, 2015
2:00 p.m.
Greater St. Luke A.M.E. Church – 78 Gordon Street, Charleston, SC 29403
Reverend Dr. Herbert Temoney, Presiding

Prelude

Processional .... Reflection Music

Viewing .... Funeral Directors

Opening Hymn .... Greater St. Luke A.M.E. Church and St. Luke A.M.E. Church Combined Choirs
"I Hear My Savior Calling" # 235

Prayer .... Reverend Robert Stokes, *Pastor of Mt. Horr A.M.E. Church, Yonges Island, SC*

Old Testament - Joshua 1: 1-7 .... Retired Presiding Elder Lorenzo T. Baker

New Testament - Roman 8: 24-33 .... Reverend John Bradley, *Pastor of St. Luke A.M.E. Church, Charleston, SC*

Hymn of Praise .... Greater St. Luke A.M.E. Church and St. Luke A.M.E. Church Combined Choirs
"There's Not A Friend"

Resolution .... *Mother* Emmanuel A.M.E. Church, Charleston, SC

Selection .... Children and Grandchildren

Remarks .... Honorable Joseph P. Riley, Jr., City of Charleston Mayor

Reflections
Class Leader – Representative *Mother* Emmanuel A.M.E. Church
Ms. Darlene Ravenal - *St. Luke A.M.E. Church*
Mr. Alfonzo Miller - *Family*
Mr. Daniel L. Simmons, Jr. - *Son*

Solo .... Ms. Rose Simmons

Family Tribute (Video Presentation)

Hymn of Preparation .... Greater St. Luke A.M.E. Church and St. Luke A.M.E. Church Combined Choirs
"The Old Ship of Zion"

Words of Comfort .... Retired Presiding Elder John Gillison

The Lord's Prayer (Chant)

Recessional .... Greater St. Luke A.M.E. Church and St. Luke A.M.E. Church Combined Choirs
"Going Up Yonder"

Postlude

Repast: Greater St. Luke A.M.E. Church Fellowship Hall

The Order of Eulogistic Services
Thursday, July 2, 2015
11:00 a.m.
Bethel A.M.E. Church – 819 Woodrow Street, Columbia, SC 29205
Presiding: Elder Novell Goff
Reverend Dr. Ronnie E. Brailsford, Pastor

Prelude

Processional...Reflection Music

Opening Hymn.............................."I Hear My Savior Calling" # 235....................................The Choir

Closing of Casket..Family

Prayer..Pastor Arthur Rogers
Pastor of New Life Church, Hampton, VA

Old Testament...Joshua 1: 1-7.............................Reverend Julius Steed
Pastor of Greater Unity A.M.E. Church, Holly Hill, SC

New Testament..Romans 8: 24-33.....................Reverend Dr. Ronnie E. Brailsford
Pastor of Bethel A.M.E. Church, Columbia, SC

Selection..New Life Church Mass Choir, Hampton, VA

Resolution...Senator John Scott, *Richland County Senate District 19*

Selection..New Life Church Mass Choir, Hampton, VA

Family Tribute (Video Presentation)

Reflections
Reverend Dr. Charles Young - *Former President of Allen University*
Dr. William Smith - *Presiding Elder of Marion District Northeast Conference*
Mr. Harrison Rearden - *Long time Neighbor*
Mr. Alfonzo Miller – *Cousin*
Reverend Michael Simmons - *Retired Interate Elder, Dayton, OH*
Mr. Daniel L. Simmons, Jr. - *Son*

Solo..Ms. Angie Stone
Nationally Acclaimed Recording Artist

Words of Comfort..Bishop E. Earl McCloud, Jr.
127th Consecrated Elected Bishop of African Methodist Episcopal Church

The Lord's Prayer (Chant)

Hymn # 321...The Choir

Recessional

Postlude

Committal, Prayer, Benediction and Interment
Fort Jackson National Cemetery
4170 Percival Road
Fort Jackson, South Carolina

Repast: Bethel A.M.E. Church Fellowship Hall

Here are the remarks that I made at Dan's Homegoings in Charleston & Columbia:

The union of my paternal great-grandparents, Frasier Simmons and Elizabeth Miller Simmons, produced several children who lived to adulthood: my great uncle Moses Simmons (Dan Simmons' Father, the oldest of his siblings, an AME Church Pastor, and known as Uncle Mose); my great uncle Pinckney Simmons, known as Uncle Butter; my great aunt Irene Simmons Benbow, known as Aunt Nugg; my grandmother Julia Simmons Miller; my great aunt Marie Simmons McCray, known as Aunt Sing; and my great uncle Benjamin Simmons.

The Miller-Simmons' family roots originated from Davis Station, SC, a rural community in Clarendon County between Manning and Summerton. The family's church roots are at historic Mt. Zion AME Church.

Of my Grandmother's siblings, Aunt Irene was the only one who remained in Clarendon County. Because of economical challenges by the end of the 1930s, the others left Clarendon County and relocated to various geographical locations: Uncle Moses and my Grandmother Julia relocated to Mullins, SC (Marion County); Uncle Pinckney relocated to Bennettsville, SC (Marlboro County); Aunt Marie relocated to Tabor City, NC; and Uncle Benjamin relocated to Florida.

Uncle Moses Simmons and his wife, Aunt Rosa Mae Alford Simmons, had three sons: Moses Jr., Ezekiel and Daniel, making them first cousins to my father and second cousins to me and my siblings. Now, some of you know the connection between Al Miller and Dan Simmons.

Most of you from the church's perspective knew Daniel Lee Simmons, Sr. as Rev. Simmons or Super Simmons, and many in the Charleston Community knew him as Mr. Simmons. But our family knew him as Dan, Daniel or Cousin Dan.

The middle name "Lee" resonated in our family as he was Daniel Lee; and my oldest sister is Mary Lee, my youngest brother is Johnny Lee, my first cousin is Kenneth Lee and another cousin was Lee Earnest and the "Lee" middle name continues.

Dan followed in his father's footsteps: he was dedicated and loyal to his family and was that driving force that linked different branches of the family together. He was considered the Family's Chief and this was exemplified through his communicating and visits. In sickness and death Dan was there.

As family we saw his service and dedication to the church; he performed his pastoral duties well. He visited and administered Holy Communion to his sick parishioners, and did the same for others when their pastors were not available, nor of service.

When he moved to Charleston in the late 1990s we became closer and in 2006 I purchased a home in his neighborhood; so we were more than family, but neighbors. Rarely a day passed when we did not converse.

Dan was a friend, a confidant, a counselor, confident, persistent, dependable, dedicated to tasks placed before him, loyal, a people's person, outspoken when the time presented itself, and had very little tolerance for foolishness. He would have made an excellent drill sergeant in the military. He gave sound advice that paid off in the long run.

He loved jazz, and was familiar with the jazz clubs around Charleston. As a tour guide, for anyone requesting a place for Jazz, Dan was the man.

We used to tease each other about my art and his cars: Dan would say, "Al, you love your pictures," indicating my art; and I would say to him, "And you love your cars," indicating his Mercedes-Benzes. It's because of Dan that I own two Mercedes-Benzes.

Thank God for his life and the contributions he made to family, the church, mankind and the world.

On the Honorable Rev. Clementa Pinckney:
Clementa's grandmother, Gracie Stevenson Broome, and my mother, Dorothy Mae Leonard Miller, are first cousins. He was a loving, caring person and a peacemaker. I miss him for that, I really do. And he was my fraternity brother (Alpha Phi Alpha Fraternity, Inc.) Knowing Clementa, he probably told Roof, the killer: "Come my brother, come join us in our Bible study. Sit right here next to me!" Nevertheless, he shot Clementa first.

Clementa grew up in Jasper County, SC, but was taken to his mother's home in Marion, SC to be buried near his mother. It was amazing to me that media from all over the world would come to the same cemetery where most of my folk are buried. After the burial, there was a repast at St. James AME Church in Marion.

On the federal trial, December 2016:
It was painful being in the courtroom and seeing people's emotions as they broke down when talking about their loved ones. What was annoying to me was that the killer commented that he was annoyed at witnessing those family members breaking down. I remember the prosecutor saying to the judge, "Well Your Honor, it was Dylann Roof who decided he wanted to go kill nine people, and these family members have the right to talk about their loved ones."

I'll Always Remember:

- *The outpouring of acts of kindness from people, their prayers and thoughts*
- *Passing by the church on tour and seeing people bringing so many flowers*
- *Family members gathering at my house to go to Clementa's funeral. I drove my tour bus to the Visitor Center and parked, and we walked to the TD Arena*
- *How there were thousands of people at Clementa's funeral. My heart went out to people who had been waiting in line since 7 am that morning, and so many couldn't get in. Several blocks of Meeting and Calhoun Sts. were blocked off*

- *Hearing President Obama sing "Amazing Grace". A Spirit went all over the place*
- *Family members gathering at my house to go to Dan's Charleston funeral, then we went to his house and got in the limos*
- *How this tragedy brought my family members closer together*
- *How a few weeks before (the shooting), Dan had been calling quite a bit, a little bit more than the norm. "Maybe Daddy sensed death," I remember Deon saying when we talked about it*
- *That almost the entire church ministerial staff was killed. It could've been a worse outcome had others attended the Bible study. Quarterly Conference was being held at the church, and the meetings ran late, so Bible study started later than usual. Some who may have stayed for it didn't because it was such a long day*
- *Asking myself over and over - Why do some White people hate Black people so much? What did we do to them?*
- *How shocked I was that they caught him (the killer) so soon*
- *How I felt when it came out that he was a racist with no remorse for what he did*
- *All the times I would get angry and would want to just kill him*
- *That I eventually realized - he's sick*
- *When the Confederate flag came down (from the statehouse grounds in Columbia, SC, July 10, 2015). All of them (the Emanuel 9) died as a sacrifice*

A Few of the Life Lessons that I've Learned:
- *Do it now, don't procrastinate and regret that you didn't do it*
- *Don't put off telling people how you feel about them*
- *Forgiveness is a thing that has to grow within you. In the killer's case, it's something that had to grow on me when I considered the source. I forgave him, but will never forget*
- *I really take life seriously now, living life to the fullest because we never know what's going to happen to us when we walk out the door, and whether we're going to come home or not*

RESURRECTION
SUNDAY
CELEBRATE THE SAVIOR
REMEMBERING THE EMANUEL 9 | HONORING THE SURVIVORS
REV. CLEMENTA PINCKNEY
CYNTHIA HURD
REV. SHARONDA COLEMAN- SINGLETON
TYWANZA SANDERS
SUSIE JACKSON
ETHEL LANCE
MYRA THOMPSON
DEPAYNE MIDDLETON-DOCTOR
REV. DANIEL SIMMONS SR.
Survivors
FELICIA SANDERS
JENNIFER BENJAMIN PINCKNEY
POLLY SHEPPARD
FAMILY & FRIENDS
HOMECOMING CELEBRATION
COMMEMORATIVE SOUVENIR JOURNAL
Dr. Gail Joyner-Fleming, Co-Chairperson
Brother Isaiah Just, Co-Chairperson
Dr. Kylon Jerome Middleton, Pastor
SUNDAY MARCH 27, 2016

Tourists Can Say the Darndest Things! 27

The Seventh Episcopal District of the African Methodist Episcopal Church of South Carolina

An Ecumenical Service
Remembering the Mother Emanuel Nine and
Honoring the Survivors & Members of Mother Emanuel AME Church

Rev. Sheronda Coleman-Singleton
Rev. Daniel Simmons, Sr.
Mr. Tywanza Sanders
Mrs. Myra Singleton Thompson
Mrs. Cynthia Graham-Hurd

Mrs. Susie Jackson
Rev. Dr. Clementa Pinckney
Rev. DePayne Middleton-Doctor
Mrs. Ethel Lance

RIGHT REVEREND RICHARD F. NORRIS
PRESIDING PRELATE
MOTHER MARY ANN NORRIS
EPISCOPAL SUPERVISOR

REV. DR. NORVEL GOFF, SR., PRESIDING ELDER, EDISTO DISTRICT
REV. DR. BETTY CLARK, PASTOR, MOTHER EMANUEL AME CHURCH

FRIDAY, JUNE 17, 2016 AT 10:00 A.M.
THE COLLEGE OF CHARLESTON
TD ARENA
301 MEETING STREET • CHARLESTON, SC 29401

Interviews with Mr. Daniel L. Simmons, Jr. (Deon) Monday night, February 1, 2016 at the home of the late Rev. Daniel L. Simmons, Sr., N. Charleston, SC & Tuesday night, March 28, 2017 via telephone
by A.M. Shinault-Small

Deon Simmons and Al Miller have a catch-up conversation at the late Rev. Daniel L. Simmons, Sr.'s home, February 1, 2016.

February 1, 2016:
AMS: Hi Deon, please tell me a little about yourself.
DLS: *I'm named after my father, but I go by Deon. I live with my family in the Hampton Roads VA area. I'm married to Arcelia Simmons and I have four children, (ages) 26, 25, 21 and 17.*

How many siblings do you have?
DLS: I have a younger sister.

AMS: How were you notified about June 17th?
DLS: *After Al asked me if I had heard from my dad, and then told me to watch the news, I began packing. I got the official news of my dad's death from the Richland County Coroner around 5 am Thursday (June 18, 2015). I was on (interstate) 95 South.*

Tourists Can Say the Darndest Things!

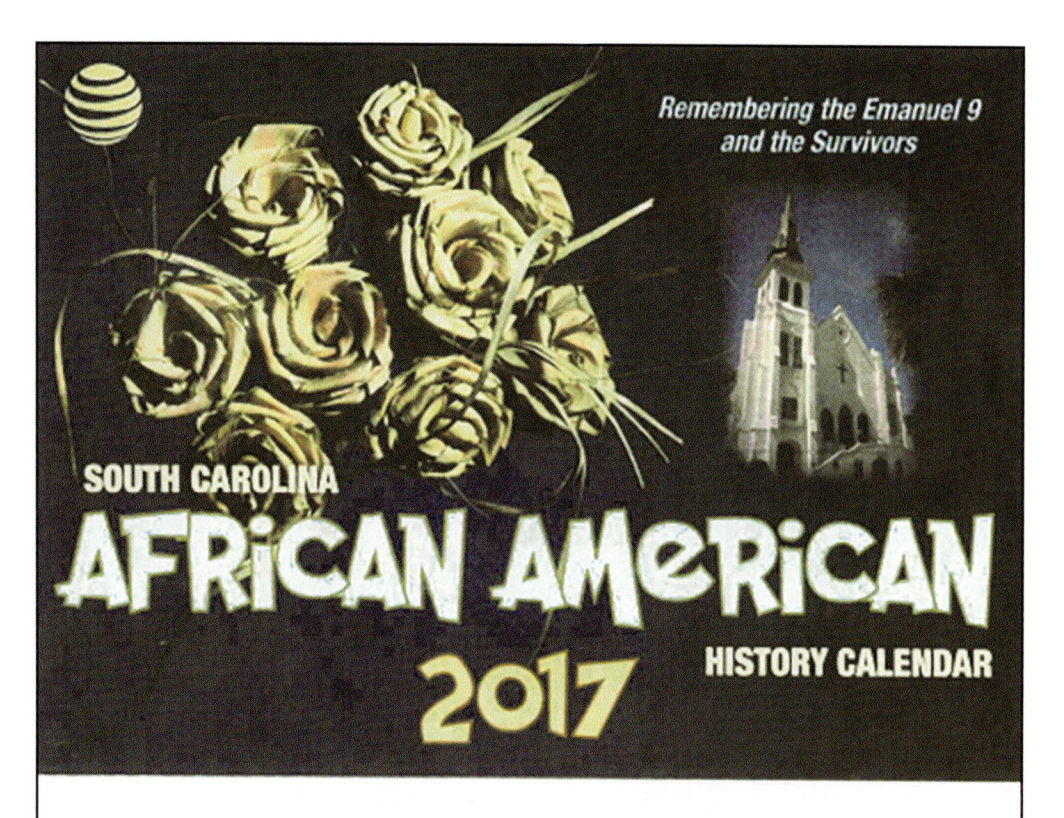

South Carolina African American 2017 History Calendar

Remembering the Emanuel 9 and the Survivors

28th Annual Unveiling Ceremony

Tuesday, October 4, 2016
7:00pm

Koger Center for the Arts
Greene St. at Assembly St., Columbia, SC

2017 Honorees

Rev. Sharonda Coleman-Singleton
Cynthia Graham Hurd
Susie J. Jackson
Ethel Lee Lance
Rev. DePayne Vontrese Middleton
Honorable Rev. Clementa Pinckney

Tywanza Kibwe Diop Sanders
Rev. Daniel L. Simmons, Sr.
Myra Singleton Thompson
Survivors
Emanuel A.M.E. Church

The late Rev. Daniel L. Simmons, Sr. stands proudly between his son Daniel L. Simmons, Jr. (Deon), on the left, & his grandson Daniel L. Simmons, III, on the right, at their Norfolk State University graduation in 2014. Photo provided by Deon Simmons

AMS: Why did you hear from the Richland Co. coroner instead of Charleston County's?
DLS: My mother is in Richland Co. and my previous address is there. He got my phone number from my mother.

AMS: What stands out to you about the last seven months or so?
DLS: The expressions of love to my family from people I didn't know, an overwhelming response of cards and memos, and the outpouring of caring and forgiveness and grace that's been expressed.

AMS: What is "Hate Won't Win"?
DLS: The "Hate Won't Win Movement" was birthed at the hearing in North Charleston and it landed on my daughter's heart. God put it on her heart to deliver it to the nation, which father would've wanted and would be very proud of his grandchildren. The Movement is a non-profit organization. We sell shirts, book speaking engagements for me and my children. We accept donations and we have a Facebook page and a website.

Tourists Can Say the Darndest Things!

AMS: How did your t-shirt come about?

DLS: *It was developed by my son, Daniel Simmons, III with "Hate Won't Win" on it. I'm proud how my children have developed and shared this message. It's our ministry. After Clementa's homegoing, family members of all of the deceased met with the president at TD Arena. A shirt was presented to him and Mrs. Obama by the family.*

President Barack Obama and First Lady Michelle Obama display the hand heart and a "Hate Won't Win" t-shirt, June 2015. Photo courtesy of the Hate Won't Win Movement.

AMS: What are some of the media outlets that y'all gave interviews to?

DLS: *Our first interview to the nation was on <u>Meet The Press</u>. Also <u>Essence</u> magazine, <u>Glamour</u> magazine, <u>Time</u>, CNN, Fox News, <u>USA Today</u> and others to honor father. We did three interviews on Father's Day (June 21st), one that night and others on Monday.*

AMS: To close out, what message would you like to share?

DLS: *God gives everyone space and room to convey His message.*

Deon Simmons' children from left to right are Daniel L. Simmons, III, Ava Simmons, Alana Simmons & Anya Simmons. They're standing in front of Mother Emanuel in June 2015 "conveying His message". Photo courtesy of the Hate Won't Win Movement

March 28, 2017:

AMS: What are your thoughts on the recent federal trial Deon?
DLS: *It was very long with all of the different phases: jury selection, motions, hearings, sentencing; four months of back and forth down the road for everything. The Department of Justice did an outstanding job. Lots of things had to be documented and redocumented to make sure there was no mistrial.*

AMS: And your thoughts on the outcome?
DLS: *It was what I expected.*

AMS: Update me on the "Hate Won't Win Movement".
DLS: *We're moving toward the second anniversary. My daughter Alana is handling everything including social media. All updates are put on the website. (https://www.hatewontwinmovement.com/)*

AMS: Thanks for your time to follow up our previous conversation over a year ago. Any final thoughts?
DLS: *What I've shared (then and now) is highlights of our experiences, not our complete experience, and there hasn't been closure yet. The prisoner is still in state custody. Any death penalty automatically can be appealed by our circuit judges. I'm looking and praying that everything goes well with no loopholes found. Again, the judge and the Dept. of Justice did a great job. There's a lot of stuff open before closure. This could take zero to ten years or longer. Nothing will be settled 'til they roll him out and strap him in the chair and do what they have to do to him.*

Portrait of the late Rev. Daniel L. Simmons, Sr., a gift that was delivered to Mother Emanuel for the Simmons family.

Editor's Note: Dylann Roof, intending to start a race war, was convicted in December 2016 on 33 federal charges relating to the 9 murders that he committed without remorse at Mother Emanuel. He was given a death sentence in January 2017. On April 10, 2017, the 23 year-old from the Columbia, SC area pleaded guilty to 13 state charges – 9 counts of murder, 3 counts of attempted murder and a weapons charge. He received 9 consecutive life sentences without parole, and no second trial will be held. Later in April, the killer was transferred to death row at Terre Haute Federal Prison in Indiana. This medium-security facility houses male inmates awaiting execution by lethal injection under the federal government. As of late April 2017, it housed a little over 1,330 inmates.

Tourists Can Say the Darndest Things!

A TRIBUTE TO MOTHER EMANUEL: AT THE CHARLESTON INTERNATIONAL AIRPORT

On April 15, 2017, the state's busiest airport unveiled a tribute and art exhibit inside the terminal. It contains two stained glass window panes, photos, a painting, a Bible opened to the Scripture that the slain persons and the survivors were studying, and the Rev. Clementa Pinckney's Bible. Nearby seating allows visitors and travelers to be able to sit, view and reflect.

These 5 foot-high stained glass window panes are the focal point of the display. They depict a Cross with 4 doves (left) & Emanuel AME Church with 5 doves (right).

CHARLESTON COUNTY AVIATION AUTHORITY
Charleston International Airport

Central Hall
Saturday, April 15, 2017
8:30 AM

Tribute Selection	*How Great Thou Art* Benjamin Seabrook, *Mt. Zion AME*
Welcome	Margaret Seidler, *CCAA Tribute Committee*
Invocation	Reverend Eric S.C. Manning, *Mother Emanuel AME*
Remembering & Honoring	Spencer Pryor, *CCAA Tribute Committee*
Charleston, Light of The World	Reverend Anthony Thompson, *Holy Trinity Reformed Episcopal, Husband of Mrs. Myra Thompson*
Reflections and Blessing of the Space	Samuel Lawrence Green, Sr. *Presiding Bishop, Seventh Episcopal District*
Benediction	Rev. Dr. Spike Coleman, *St. Andrews Presbyterian Coastal Crisis Chaplaincy*
Selection	*Amazing Grace*
Closing Words	Helen Hill, *CCAA Tribute Committee*

Tourists Can Say the Darndest Things! 35

Family members were given these lovely tags at the Charleston International Airport's Emanuel 9 Tribute unveiling on April 15, 2017.

Charlestonian Adriene Buist viewed the tribute when she flew home for a visit in early May 2017, and then viewed it again before leaving. She commented: "It's truly mind blowing how a place of peace and love was the receiver of hate and violence. Thank God! Love Conquers All!"

SATURDAY, JUNE 17, 2017 SECOND YEAR OBSERVANCE

Above - The march observing the 2nd anniversary of the Mother Emanuel tragedy departed from Marion Square, 1 block from the church. The Rev. Eric Manning, Emanuel's pastor, is on the left behind the "Hate Won't Win" sign (wearing clerical collar); to his right, Charleston mayor John Tecklenburg; to his right, Alana Simmons, Hate Won't Win Movement Founder & CEO & granddaughter of the late Rev. Daniel L. Simmons, Sr.; and directly behind her, her father Daniel L. Simmons, Jr. (wearing sunglasses). Jeffrey Robinson, with the ACLU, was the keynote speaker at the commemorative markers unveiling program that occurred immediately after the march. He is 2nd from the right (jacket on arm). **Center Left -** Daniel L. Simmons, Jr. (Deon) & Polly Sheppard, a survivor of the shooting, greeted each other before the march. **Bottom Left -** One of the messages displayed during the march. **Center Right -** The opened front gates of Mother Emanuel. The floral tributes were left by the public. When the march paused in front of the church, the church's bells filled the air in tribute for several minutes. **Bottom Right -** After the musical tribute, a group of girls processed through the open gates, went up the front stairway from both sides, and released 9 roses. Then, 9 doves were released that flew westwardly in unison.

Tourists Can Say the Darndest Things!

SECOND ANNUAL ECUMENICAL SERVICE

The following five pages are from the Ecumenical Worship Service program, held at 1:00 pm on Saturday, June 17, 2017 at the Charleston Gaillard Center.

SECOND ANNUAL ECUMENICAL WORSHIP SERVICE

ORDER OF SACRED WORSHIP SERVICE
WORSHIP LEADER: REVEREND ERIC S.C. MANNING, PASTOR

Musical Interlude	Charleston Symphony String Ensemble
The Prelude	
The Processional	All Hail the Power of Jesus Name
The Call to Worship	Reverend Dr. Spike Coleman
	PASTOR, ST. ANDREWS PRESBYTERIAN

Leader: Lord, we have so much to thank You for, so many wonderful blessings that you have given to each of the families who had to endure.
Response: That's why we Trust you O Lord.

Leader: You have brought us through every valley, and over every mountain top experience.
Response: That's why we Love you O Lord.

Leader: You have given us a new day, a day that is filled with new grace and new mercy.
Response: That's why we Praise you O Lord.

ALL: We lift our hands, our hearts, and our minds to you now and humbly ask that you replenish and restore each of us. Amen.

The Hymn of Praise AMEC Hymn # 364   Reverend Randolph Miller
PASTOR, NICHOLS CHAPEL AME CHURCH

MY HOPE IS BUILT

1. My hope is built on nothing less Than Jesus blood and righteousness; I dare not trust the sweetest frame, But wholly lean on Jesus name. **REFRAIN:** *On Christ, the solid rock, I stand; All other ground is sinking sand, All other ground is sinking sand.*

2. When darkness veils His lovely face, I rest on His unchanging grace; In every high and story tale, My anchor holds within the veil. **REFRAIN:** *On Christ, the solid rock, I stand; All other ground is sinking sand, All other ground is sinking sand.*

3. His oath His covenant, His blood Support me in the whelming flood; When all around my soul gives way, He then is all my hope and stay. **REFRAIN:** *On Christ, the solid rock, I stand; All other ground is sinking sand, All other ground is sinking sand.*

4. When He shall come with trumpet sound, O may I then in Him be found! Dressed in His righteousness alone, Faultless to stand before the throne! **REFRAIN:** *On Christ, the solid rock, I stand; All other ground is sinking sand, All other ground is sinking sand.*

The Ecumenical Prayer	Reverend Alford Zadig, Jr. RECTOR, ST. MICHAELS CHURCH
The Choral Response	ALL
Musical Selection	Mother Emanuel Combined Choir
The Scripture Lesson Psalm 46	Reverend Dr. J. Eric Skidmore SC STATE POLICE CHAPLAIN

THE PRAYERS FOR THE EMANUEL "9" FAMILIES AND SURVIVORS

Musical Selections Performed by Charleston Symphony Orchestra

Reverend Clementa C. Pinckney
Mrs. Jennifer Pinckney
The Pinckney Family - Reverend Dr. Kylon Middleton
PASTOR, MT. ZION AME CHURCH, CHARLESTON, SC

Reverend Daniel L. Simmons, Sr.
The Simmons Family - Reverend Dr. Herbert Temoney
PASTOR, GREATER ST. LUKE AME CHURCH, CHARLESTON, SC

Reverend Sharonda Coleman Singleton
The Singleton Family - Reverend Cecelia D. Armstrong
ASSOCIATE PASTOR, ST. JAMES PRESBYTERIAN CHURCH, USA

Reverend DePayne Middleton
The Middleton Family - Reverend Waltrina N. Middleton
ASSOCIATE DEAN, ANDREW RANKIN MEMORIAL CHAPEL, HOWARD UNIVERSITY, WASHINGTON, DC

Mrs. Myra Singleton Thompson
The Thompson Family - Reverend S. Marshall Blalock
PASTOR, FIRST BAPTIST CHURCH, CHARLESTON, SC

Mrs. Cynthia Graham Hurd
The Hurd Family - Reverend David Bowman
ASSISTANT - PASTORAL CARE, ST. MICHAELS CHURCH, CHARLESTON, SC

Mrs. Susie Jackson
The Jackson Family - Reverend Dr. Myra D. Meggett
PASTOR, GREATER BETHEL AME CHURCH, JAMES ISLAND, SC

Mrs. Ethel Lance
The Lance Family - Reverend Sharon Risher

Mr. Tywanza Sanders
Mrs. Felicia Sanders
The Sanders Family - Reverend Cress Darwin
PASTOR, SECOND PRESBYTERIAN CHURCH, CHARLESTON, SC

Mrs. Polly Sheppard
The Sheppard Family - Reverend Eric S.C. Manning
PASTOR, MOTHER EMANUEL AME CHURCH, CHARLESTON, SC

Mother Emanuel AME Church Family
Reverend James Keaton
PASTOR, MORRIS BROWN AME CURCH, CHARLESTON, SC

Musical Selection	Mother Emanuel AME Church Choir
Mother Emanuel Praise Dancers	
Musical Selection	Mount Moriah Baptist Choir
Presentation of the Ecumenical Speaker	Presiding Elder Norvel Goff, Sr.
	EDISTO DISTRICT SC CONFERENCE
Musical Selection	Mount Moriah Baptist Choir
Ecumenical Message	Reverend Dr. Joel C. Gregory

The Hymn of Christian Discipleship Hymn - AME Hymn # 226

AMAZING GRACE

1. Amazing grace! how sweet the sound, That saved a wretch like me! I once was lost, but now am found, Was blind, but now I see,
2. 'Twas grace that taught my heart to fear, And grace my fears relieved; How precious did that grace appear The hour I first believed!
3. Through many dangers, toils, and snares, I have already come; 'Tis grace hath brought me safe thus far, And grace will lead me homes.
4. The Lord has promised good to me, His word my hope secures; He will my shield and portion be. As long as life endures.

Leadership Awards	Councilman William D. Gregorie
Special Family Presentations	Mr. Leroy Campbell
Remarks	

Mayor John Tecklenburg
MAYOR, CHARLESTON, SC

Governor Henry McMaster
GOVERNOR, SOUTH CAROLINA

Bishop Samuel L. Green, Sr.
PRESIDING BISHOP, 7TH EPISCOPAL DISTRICT

The Doxology	
The Benediction	Bishop Samuel L. Green, Sr.
The Recessional	

The painting Bible Study, depicts the legacy of the Charleston Emanuel Nine and God's indelible grace that engraved each of their names on the palms of His hands - the Honorable Reverend Clementa Pinckney, Reverend Sharonda Coleman-Singleton, Cynthia Hurd, Tywanza Sanders, Ethel Lance, Susie Jackson, Reverend Daniel Simmons, Sr., Myra Thompson, and Reverend Depayne Middleton.

The painting tells the story of an old-fashioned, backwoods creek baptism. Behind the woman emerging from the water, trees bloom in vibrant shades of magenta, fuchsia, and violet. The space between the trees is illuminated by the truth and light of God's word, Matthew 13, the parable of the Sower, the same passage the Charleston Emanuel Nine were studying the night their lives were tragically taken.

Infused in the right side of the collage, is an example of seeds that fell on infertile ground, seeds that had no depth of earth, shallow roots that left them scorched and withered. In 1963, the moment a bomb struck the 16th Street Baptist Church in Birmingham, Alabama, the clock stopped. The clock symbolizes infertile ground.

The fruits of seeds that fell on fertile ground are represented on the left side of the collage by the calendar from 1964, the year Dr. Martin Luther King, Jr. and other Civil Rights leaders witnessed President Lyndon B. Johnson signing the Civil Rights Act, a step towards freedom and equality for all. Dr. Martin Luther King, Jr. sowed and watered the seeds. God grew and multiplied them, yielding a crop thirty, sixty, one-hundred times that which he had planted in faith, demonstrating what God can do with a fertile heart.

Embedded in the background, you will also find the steeple of Mother Emanuel African Methodist Episcopal Church, the heart of the Holy City, now a symbol of unity and hope, of strength and forgiveness, of light in the darkness, of triumph over tragedy. The collage is designed to document and to teach.

Two men stand on either side of the Woman being baptized, helping her to her feet. Although she is still weak, she is filled with the joy of God's promises and the hope of the resurrection. The men are a reminder that no matter what we might be going through in life, whether it's joy or pain, we are never alone. The woman has been give wings to help her ascend to her new beginning, her new way of thinking, her new way of doing, her new way of being.

Her dress bears the black and white images of each of the Emanuel Nine. She carries pieces of them in her soul - pastor, senator, grandmother, mother, father, daughter, son, sister, brother, coach, barber, poet, entrepreneur, librarian, lover of jazz, veteran, custodian, speech therapist, teacher, guidance counselor, choir signer, leader, beloved. Next to each one of them are scriptures and quotes to give each a voice, to give us counsel, understanding, and direction.

"No amount of money could ever give me the joy and the reward I've received from being given this mission, from being led by God to use my gifts to create, to love, and to serve. I have been handsomely repaid by knowing I was chosen for such a time as this. I hope all who help to keep the voice, the spirit, and the intentions of the Charleston Emanuel Nine alive will receive the love that only God can put inside of us. Nothing can be greater than that."
Leroy Campbell

A limited number of reproductions will be made from this sixty-by-seventy-two-inch original painting, each one numbered and signed. In addition, nine of these commemorative-edition, embellished, framed prints will be given to the next of kin of each of the victim's family.

Each month a portion of the proceeds from the sales of the reproductions of Bible Study will be donated to a worthy cause or foundation on behalf of each of the Emanuel Nine.

Tourists Can Say the Darndest Things!

41

Looking Back

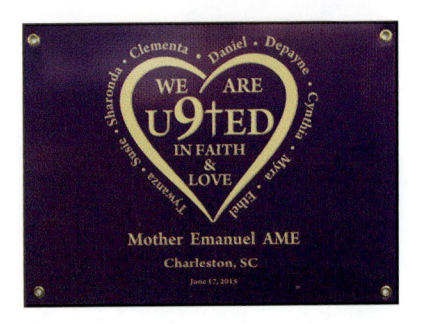

Left This banner with a rich purple background & gold lettering was attached to the front of Mother Emanuel for many months.
Right Mother Emanuel on the front eastern side on the afternoon of 6-19-15.

Left Tributes blanketed the front of the church on 7-1-15, photo courtesy of Debbie S. Kines. **Right** Many well-wishers autographed the fire hydrants and crape myrtle tree trunks located in front of the church.

Left This flower arrangement decorated the church's front sign-board in Aug. 2015. **Right** A message that had been setting on the lower church windowsill was paired with a bouquet bearing the names of the Emanuel 9 on the ribbons.

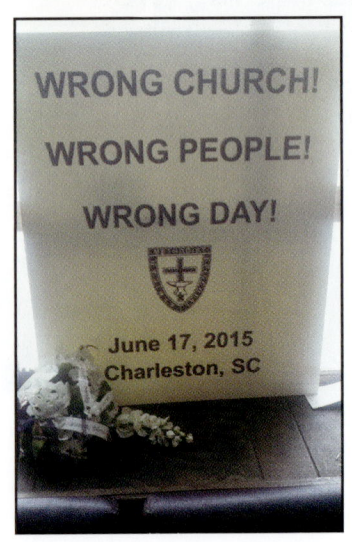

Tourists Can Say the Darndest Things! 43

In Retrospect

Charleston City Council unanimously passed a resolution to rename a portion of Calhoun St. as "Mother Emanuel Way Memorial District" in Sept. 2015. A church member who's on City Council introduced the resolution.

These are some of the tributes that were placed in front of the church in June 2016 during the one-year anniversary of the murders.

Left The front cover of the Rev. Senator Clementa C. Pinckney's funeral program. President Barack Obama offered the Eulogy. The order of service follows on the next 2 pages. **Right** The Rev. Pinckney's gravesite at St. James AME Church cemetery, Marion, SC.

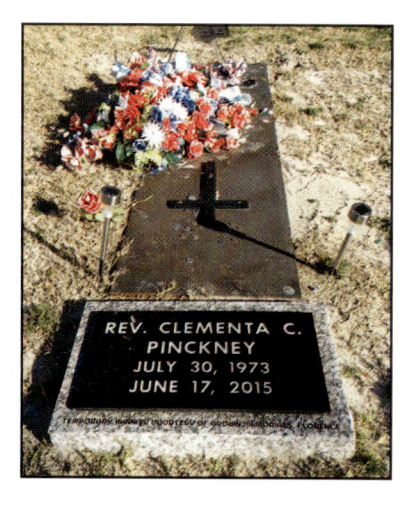

The Order of Celebration
Friday, June 26, 2015
11:00 a.m.
TD Arena – Charleston, South Carolina

Pre-Service Music 11:00 a.m. -11:30 a.m.
Lowcountry Voices - Sandra Barnhardt & Nathan L. Nelson

Musical Prelude ....Medley of Spiritual Songs

The Processional 11:45 a.m.

The Call to Worship.. The Right Reverend John Richard Bryant
Senior Bishop of the African Methodist Episcopal Church
Presiding Prelate of the Fourth Episcopal District of the AME Church

Musical Selection .... "He's Done So Much for Me"............. *Mother* Emanuel AME Church Choir

Reflections from the State Capitol..Chaplain James I. St. John
Chaplain South Carolina State Senate

The Honorable Gerald Malloy, *Senate District 29*
Chesterfield, Darlington, Lee, and Marlboro Counties

The Honorable Reverend Joseph Neal, *House District 70*
Richland and Sumter Counties

Episcopal Expressions... The Right Reverend John Richard Bryant
Senior Bishop of the African Methodist Episcopal Church
Presiding Prelate of the Fourth Episcopal District of the AME Church

Reflections from the Clergy..The Reverend Dr. Ronnie Elijah Brailsford
Pastor, Bethel AME Church

The Reverend Dr. John H. Gillison
Retired, Presiding Elder

The Reverend Dr. George F. Flowers
Executive Director, AME Global Witness & Ministry

Mother **Emanuel Church Resolution and Tribute**..Mother Emanuel AME Church

Musical Selection .... "How Excellent" .... *Mother* Emanuel AME Church Choir

Acknowledgement of Civic and Religious Leaders... Sister Tylaunda Corbin

Musical Tribute ...."Permit Now, Oh Lord: My Soul To Enter"................................Dr. Greg McPherson

Reflections from the Friends, the Church, & the Family:

The Reverend Chris Vaughn, Friend
Brother William Dudley Gregorie, Church
The Reverend Dr. Kylon Jerome Middleton, Spiritual Brother
Brother Ronnie Johnson, Cousin
The Reverend Donald Sheftal, Cousin

The Order of Eulogistic Services

Eulogistic Services Officiated By:
The Reverend Dr. Norvel Goff, Sr., Presiding Elder
The Edisto District of the South Carolina Annual Conference
Seventh Episcopal District of the African Methodist Episcopal Church

Opening Selection .... "My Help" .... Lowcountry Voices - Sandra Barnhardt & Nathan L. Nelson

Opening Sentences .... The Reverend Dr. Norvel Goff, Sr.
Presiding Elder, The Edisto District

The Hymn of Comfort
The Choir and Congregation .... "It is Well" .... The Reverend Dr. Charles Watkins
Pastor, Morris Brown AME Church

The Invocation .... The Reverend Joseph Postell
Presiding Elder, The Lancaster District

The Anthem .... "O God Our Help in Ages Past" .... Mother Emanuel AME Church Choir

The Old Testament Scripture .... Reverend Dr. Lawrence Gordon
Pastor, Macedonia AME Church

The Epistle .... The Reverend Gregory M. Kinsey
Pastor, Saint John AME Church

The Gospel .... The Reverend Dr. Juenarrl Keith
Presiding Elder, The Mount Pleasant District

Eulogistic Hymn .... "My Hope Is Built" .... Mother Emanuel AME Church Choir

Eulogy .... President Barack Obama
President of the United States of America

Prayer of Comfort .... The Reverend Joseph Darby
Presiding Elder, The Beaufort District

Acknowledgement on Behalf of the Family .... The Reverend Dr. Chris Leevy Johnson
Leevy's Funeral Home

Recessional .... "You've Got to Answer to Your Name" .... Pastor H. E. Dixon & Company

Postlude

Committal, Prayer, Benediction and Interment
Saint James A.M.E. Church Cemetery
Marion, South Carolina

4 | Gullah + Geechee = Gullah Geechee

"We're here to hear all about Gullah and Geechee." "Will we get to meet the Gullah People?" "We heard the Gullahs live on the islands only." "My Grandmother came to NY from Charleston, and she had that funny dialect and always ate rice." "My wife and I saw a documentary about Gullah on the PBS station in our city." "What's the difference between Gullah and Geechee?" "Where are the Gullahs?" "Where are the Geechees?" "We heard them speaking that Geechee talk." "Look at (Supreme Court Justice) Clarence Thomas; he grew up Gullah Geechee in Pinpoint, GA outside of Savannah." These are just the tip of the iceberg of the many questions asked and remarks made through the years about Gullah Geechee culture.

Gullah is an English-based creole - a combination of West African languages, English and English Caribbean influences. Geechee refers to native African Americans in the four-state area from southern coastal NC, down through the SC and GA coasts to northern coastal FL and extending inland about thirty miles. Although some use the terms interchangeably, Gullah refers to the language and Geechee refers to the people mentioned above. The term "Gullah Geechee" has become an all-inclusive key word to describe the language, people and the Old World culture that was transferred by the West Africans who were enslaved then forcibly relocated to North American southeast coastal areas. Their traditions and folkways, including language, were passed down through the generations and are still present among their descendants.

Another common question is about the origin of "Gullah" and "Geechee". Well, some believe that Gullah evolved from the word Angola, the southwest African country where a substantial number of enslaved people originated. Others believe that Gullah is a form of Gola, an ethnic group that has roots in Sierra Leone and in what's now Liberia. Geechee, many believe, derived from the name of the Kissi people of Guinea, Sierra Leone and Liberia. Interstate 16 outside of Savannah, GA crosses the Ogeechee River; others believe that the term derived from the river's name. In coastal GA, before the term Gullah Geechee became popular, folks primarily called themselves Low Land Geechees and Salt Water Geechees; those who lived more inland usually called themselves High Land Geechees and Fresh Water Geechees. Before the term Gullah Geechee became popular in coastal SC, folks generally called themselves Gullah because Geechee was considered to be a put-down.

Locals say that if someone called a SC native a Geechee as late as thirty or so years ago, that could easily spark a fight. It was as bad to them as telling someone "Your mama". I warned visitors from time to time when I became a tour guide, "Be very careful calling people Geechees, you may get punched in the mouth." It seems that since Alex Haley published his famous book *Roots* followed by the production of the TV mini-series, Blacks nationwide began searching for their roots and seeking out non-distorted historical info and cultural experiences, leading to a full embrace of their ancestry, Gullah Geechees included.

Concerning foodways, some of the foods that were introduced to America from West Africa are: okra, watermelon, peanuts (also called goobers), black-eyed peas and benne (sesame) seeds. Examples of traditional Gullah Geechee favorites are red rice (rice cooked with tomatoes or in tomato sauce); okra soup; perlo (rice+meat or rice+a vegetable(s) that's seasoned with meat, traditionally pork. Some call this one-pot dish prioleau, pronounced *PRAY-low*); rice wine; gumbo (vegetable stew); jelly cake (layer cake with jelly, jam or preserves between the layers); fried fish with the heads on; shrimp and grits; and potato poon (sweet potato pone), to name a few.

Gullah Geechees have been called "rice eaters", often said and received as a put-down. Considering that rice was a major cash crop for almost 200 years, and considering that countless West Africans from rice-growing areas on the continent were enslaved, brought to the coastal South and forced to impart their knowledge and skills with no compensation - of course folks would eat the grains. Think about it - rice is a carbohydrate, and carbs will fill an empty belly. The flip side though is that a plate full of carbs like, for instance, black-eye peas seasoned with a ham hock served over white rice, macaroni & cheese, potato salad, and a hunk of cake alongside some barbecue ribs will fill you up nicely and surely "eat good" as Gullah Geechees would say, but look out for your blood sugar, blood pressure and cholesterol counts meanwhile.

Mr. Graham from OH who was traveling with his sisters one year commented, "Yep, our grandmother came from SC to OH and she was a Geechee, and she loved her rice." Mr. Tisdale of Pittsburg, PA followed up with, "My father came from Andrews, SC and met my mother who was a northerner. He demanded she cook rice everyday. My mother hated it at first but cooked it to please him and keep the peace."

Tourists Can Say the Darndest Things!

Enslaved West Africans introduced okra (above left) and peanuts (above right) to the US. Many of the dishes made from these and other introduced foodstuff have become a vital part of the American culinary experience.

The Gullah Geechee Cultural Heritage Corridor is a twenty-seven county area spread along the coast from southern NC to northern FL and extending about thirty miles inland. Only partial areas of some counties are included. The corridor was designated by an act of Congress in October 2006 as a part of the National Heritage Areas Act of the same year. The governing body is a fifteen-person commission with reps from NC, SC, GA and FL who are appointed by the US Secretary of Interior. Its purpose is to recognize the contributions made by Gullah Geechee people to American history and culture and to assist private and public entities with interpreting and preserving Gullah Geechee heritage.

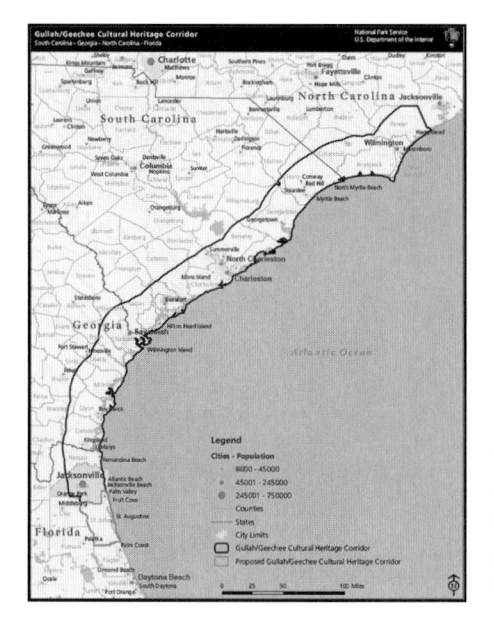

The shaded area on the right side of the map shows the 4-state Gullah Geechee Cultural Heritage Corridor. From the GGCHC website: http://www.gullahgeecheecorridor.org/index.php/heritage-corridor

Here are some very common misconceptions about Gullah Geechee people and the culture:

- Gullah Geechee people live in remote and secluded communities where visitors can go to observe and interact with them. Their day-to-day lifestyle includes living & performing tasks like people "did during slavery time"
- Gullah Geechee people live on an island(s) only reachable by boat
- There's a Gullah Island located in the Charleston area
- Gullah Geechee people are short & dark-skinned, uneducated and speak broken English
- Gullah Geechee people eat rice sandwiches, and they practice magic
- Gullah Geechee people only live along the SC and GA coasts
- All South Carolinians & all Georgians are Gullah Geechee
- Gullah Geechee people are from Jamaica
- Gullah Geechee people will stab a person without hesitation if they are angered

A lady from James Island once said, "We are all Gullah Geechee; today many have nice homes; well educated with our degrees; we are doctors, lawyers and professional people. Yes, we still love our rice and other Gullah dishes; we love our crab cracks and oyster roasts; we still love to hunt and fish and still cherish many of the old beliefs passed down from our foreparents. Many enjoy the culture in more sophisticated ways."

African American linguist Dr. Lorenzo Dow Turner (1890-1972) taught summer school at South Carolina State College (now University) located in Orangeburg in 1929. The NC native heard some students talk to each other in what sounded like broken English, and he was very intrigued. Professor Turner launched onto a path of discovery that took him throughout SC & GA interviewing and recording Gullah Geechee residents, to the University of London's School of Oriental and African Studies to learn various African languages, to Yale to study Arabic, then to Brazil to research surviving West African languages. In 1949, he published <u>Africanisms in the Gullah Dialect</u> that showcased his years of devoted research that connected many of the dots between the unique speaking patterns of

southeast coastal African Americans to various West African languages. Also, Dr. Turner's research proved that along with retaining much of their native languages, enslaved Africans also retained more of their traditions than previously thought. These traditions were continued on this side of the Atlantic and were diligently passed down through family lines.

Previously shown This is the cover of the 1974 edition of Dr. Turner's book, published by his widow Lois Turner. It was reprinted for the fourth time in 2002.

TOURISTS CAN SAY THE DARNDEST THINGS!

Oprah Winfrey bought a house in Charleston on Legare (pronounced La GREE) Street. (False)

President John F. Kennedy hooked up with Marilyn Monroe in Charleston. (It's been said that they rendezvoused at the former Sheraton Hotel overlooking the river at The Battery, now condos called the Fort Sumter House.)
"He (JFK) sure did have a good view!" one visitor said.
"He (JFK) probably wasn't even looking out at the water," responded someone else.

John C. Calhoun was a Black man and Lena Horne was his granddaughter. Some have said that Lena was his great-great niece. (?)

Enslaved Africans were sold at the City Market on Market Street. (False)

"You don't have to sugarcoat any of the Black history for this gray-haired White woman!"

Historic Charleston Foundation tells residents what colors to paint their houses. (HCF doesn't do this, but the City's Board of Architectural Review – BAR – has to approve exterior colors on structures in the historic districts.)

Geechees are short dark-skinned African Americans who reside in the country and still live "like they did in slavery time". (False)

5 | Da Burra aka The Borough aka Ansonborough

ANSONBOROUGH TODAY IS BORDERED ON THE NORTH BY CALHOUN ST., WEST BY King St., south by Market St. and east by Concord St. It was the first suburb in Charles Towne. Named for Captain George Anson, it's said that he won enough money at sea in one single card game to purchase a large tract of land. The captain's duties were to control the Carolina waters from pirate attacks. George and Anson Sts. that he named after himself still exist. Most of the structures in Ansonborough were built after 1838 because the Great Fire of that year destroyed much of the suburb. The former suburbs of Middlesex, Rhettsbury and the Laurens Lands were absorbed into present-day Ansonborough, and as mentioned in Chapter One, a portion of the area was known to some local African Americans as "Da Burra" and to others as "The Borough".

One of the notable properties in Ansonborough was Harleston-Boags Funeral Home, adjacent to Mother Emanuel AME Church. It was relocated from Meeting St. to 121 Calhoun St. in 1914 into a newly-constructed building. The business had been founded in 1896 by African American brothers Edwin G. Harleston and Robert Harleston, and

This 2010 photo of Harleston-Boags Funeral Home came out very uniquely. Look closely, & in addition to a portion of the building, you can see a reflection of my tour bus in the center & a female hand holding a camera at the far right.

they named their business Harleston Brothers Funeral Home. Edwin Harleston was a successful rice planter and sea captain. For years, the funeral home only accepted light-skinned Blacks until it was taken over by new ownership in the 1970s, becoming Harleston-Boags Funeral Home. One of the family members, the late Edwina Harleston Whitlock, was quoted as saying, "We did not do business with any Blacks who were darker than we were." Edwina's remarks usually cause stunning reactions. The skin-color class system isn't new to most Blacks; however, it's shocking and disturbing to know that some Blacks not only discriminated against the living, but also against the dead! It really "took the cake" when a visitor asked, "You mean they even discriminated against dead folk?" A White tourist proclaimed, "So Al, not only did Blacks have problems with Whites discriminating against them, but Blacks had problems with each other." Despite the fact that Harleston Brothers Funeral Home had the reputation of conducting business only with a light-skinned clientele, Edwin Harleston's son Edwin Augustus Harleston was a very gifted visual artist who started the local chapter of the NAACP and served as its president. Harleston-Boags Funeral Home went out of business in 2013. The owners sold the property, and the new owner(s) renovated the structures and had been advertising them for mixed use with a high price tag, indicative of the skyrocketing price of real estate on the peninsula that's unaffordable for many.

Author Edward Ball wrote two books documenting the connection between the White Balls and the Black Harlestons - *Slaves in the Family* (1998) and *The Sweet Hell Inside* (2001). In *Slaves in the Family*, Ball reveals the story of his family's slave-owning past and his search for the descendants of the people his ancestors enslaved. Six generations of the Ball family owned over twenty rice plantations along the Cooper River in an area near Charleston from the late 1690s to the end of the Civil War. It is believed that thousands of Africans and African Americans were enslaved by the Balls and that today there are at least 75,000-100,000 of their descendants living in America. Ball has made contact and met descendants of his family's enslaved African Americans, and many are his cousins. Because of Ball's research and record keeping by members of the Ball family, many Blacks were afforded the opportunity to trace their roots.

Many comments have been made on the tour bus about reading *Slaves in the Family* and about Ball's appearance on the Oprah Winfrey Show. "If Oprah likes your book, it becomes a part of her book club. She encourages thousands of viewers to read these books and some of the authors become instant millionaires," one visitor reported some years ago. So Mr. Tour Guide couldn't resist presenting his future book promotion: "And when my book is released, please pray 'on bended knees' that Oprah will read it and have me on her show. The world will become knowledgeable about Charleston and its visitors. I can hear Oprah saying, 'Now tell me all about those tourists and Charleston.'

I attended a book signing on February 19, 1998 for *Slaves in the Family,* and I'm proud to have an autographed copy. It was standing room only at the Avery

Research Center for African American History and Culture on 125 Bull St. here in Charleston. Some of the comments that I heard were: "He told everything in the book, including about some of his male relatives who had babies with Black women," "He just told the truth," and "I'm sure some of his relatives hate his guts for revealing everything."

Edward Ball's second intriguing book, *The Sweet Hell Inside*, tells the story of his Black cousins, the Harlestons, and their connection to the Balls and their rise to fame and fortune in the segregated South, with recollections by the late Edwina Harleston Whitlock, the family historian. One tourist said, "Oh, what a wonderful interesting, true story of an elite Black family of Charleston, South Carolina who lived better than many White Charlestonians. No stone was left unturned; all the family's dirty laundry was also revealed in the book."

"Al, please repeat the names of the books by Edward Ball," requested several visitors as they scrambled to get a pen and paper to jot the info down. "*Slaves in the Family* and *The Sweet Hell Inside*," responded Mr. Tour Guide. I've mentioned to many that in the event after the tour they go online and discover a third book written by Ball, *Peninsula of Lies*, it may be a turnoff, but I'll take a moment to tell about it to avoid e-mails accusing me of not sharing the scoop about it.

Peninsula of Lies has a totally different twist from Ball's other books. It's a true story, a piece of Charleston's history that many Charlestonians remember, and some would like to forget. It's about Dawn Langley Simmons, a British writer who settled in Charleston in the early 1960s and became the focus of an unusual sex and racial scandal. Born in England as a male, Gordon Langley Hall underwent one of the first sex change operations at Johns Hopkins University Hospital in 1968 to have a gender change. Months later she, now named Dawn, falls in love with a young Black mechanic, John Paul Simmons, and they eventually marry at her mansion at 56 Society St. Not only was the public marriage of this interracial couple the talk of the town, but so was Dawn's pregnant appearance and her later caring for their daughter, Natasha. The story has been immediately interrupted mainly by inquiring women about the news of the daughter: "Mr. Miller, stop! Where did the baby come from?" or "How did she have a baby?" Mr. Tour Guide has usually responded, "Where do all babies come from? I'm not telling, you need to read the book." One man said, "Yes, I bet Dawn wore that pillow well." My friend DeEthel H. Brown remembers the couple: "Dawn looked better as a man; she looked like hell as a woman." Whenever I share DeEthel's recollection, everyone gets a good chuckle.

Now back to Harleston-Boags Funeral Home. It is said that the house at the back of the property was built by Mr. Harleston for his mistress who had two daughters for him. He and his "regular" family lived in the three-story front house which included the funeral home. One of the Harleston cousins said to Mr. Tour Guide at church once, "The mistress also spent time in the big house." I love telling this story to see women's reactions. Nikki, a young woman, protested,

"I would not have put up with that, being Mrs. Harleston." Mr. Tour Guide responded, "Just calm down, you didn't live back then and you really don't know what you would have tolerated." In 2007 when I told this story, Celestine mentioned, "I would not have tolerated that," and another woman said, "Me too, I would not have put up with that either," and it continued with yet another woman saying, "Me three," and those comments made it up to "Me six".

Upon heading east on Calhoun St. and after crossing through the intersection of East Bay St., 35 and 35 ½ Calhoun St. are visible on the right. A sign next to the houses discusses their history and their cultural link to this section of Ansonborough.

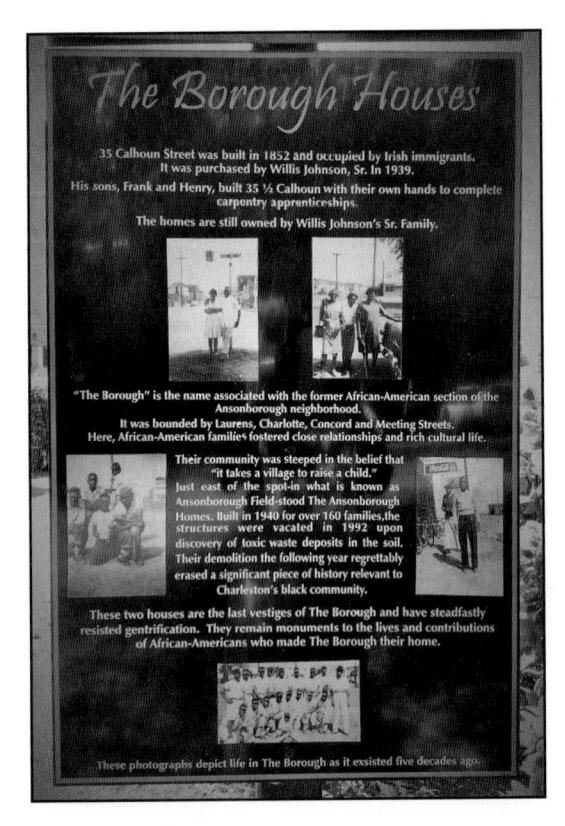

As the bus crosses Washington Street, the thirteen-acre tract of land to the right between Washington and Concord Sts. is known as Ansonborough Field, former site of Ansonborough Homes. Mrs. Smalls, who grew up in The Borough and migrated to NY in the 1960s commented, "I remember when the projects were here. And I also remember my sister telling me that the City of Charleston told the tenants that the soil was contaminated. The City promised to move them out, treat the soil, and have them return to their homes. It never happened. What a shame; all the buildings were demolished." Today the evolving development is very obvious in that area: the South Carolina Aquarium, a parking garage, Liberty Square, where visitors board boats to Fort Sumter; the former Imax Theater, condos, offices, shops, the City's Maritime Center and the future site of the International African American Museum, scheduled to open in 2019.

Many who have returned to Charleston through the years remember the Ansonborough projects. Then the on-bus conversation usually heads toward public housing: Malcolm from Cincinnati, OH said, "Some low income housing projects in my city were torn down to make room for condominiums." Leroy, a native of Orangeburg, SC, said, "I'm sure the Mayor and the City did not intend to move the residents back. Look at the location! This is prime real estate, and I know some of the residents could look out their windows and see the Cooper River." Mr. Singleton from Plainfield, NJ, who spoke with a Caribbean accent, said in 2004, "There's no way in today's society that the City of Charleston or any city would let prime property like this go to "waste". The City just made good use of it." There are different attitudes and opinions about public housing: Mr. and Mrs. Sumner agreed that some residents of public housing depend too much on the system. "Some people in the projects wear finer clothes and drive finer cars than some ordinary working people," exclaimed Mr. West from Staten Island, NY. He went on to say, "The intent of public housing years ago was to help those, especially families, to have a place to stay until they were able to find affordable housing. I know many folks who grew up in the projects but later progressed to owning their own homes." Mrs. Vidal bluntly said, "Some people have an attitude that all public housing tenants are a bunch of young Black women on welfare with lots of babies who don't want to work. That may be true in some cases, but many White women are also on welfare. Some of these people are good people, some make very little money, some are on fixed incomes and some are disabled." A farmer from the Midwest said in 2001, "I managed to survive. There are lots of farmers getting government subsidies, and that's just the sophisticated way of receiving welfare. Everybody wants a piece of the pie." And the tour continues....

A large section of The Borough was erased in 1968 when many structures were either moved to other locations in the city or demolished to make room for the construction of the Gaillard Municipal Auditorium on Calhoun St. between Anson and Alexander Sts., as we discussed in Chapter One. Herb Frazier, local author and marketing professional, grew up in The Borough. He vividly remembers some of the sights that he saw regularly in the area: a corner store, a shoe store that he peeked in the window of on the way to and from Buist Elementary School, a bar with a red neon Miller High Light sign in the window, a liquor store and Peter Pavalatos' grocery store that locals called "Nasty Pete". Frazier says that his grandmother didn't allow him to go through The Arch, as it was called then, 85 Calhoun St., the only structure that was not moved or razed. However, one day he ignored the mandate and snuck through the archway. He recalls three-tiered tenements and a strong urine smell.

Because Da Burra had its share of crime, locals often referred to it as "The Rotten Borough", and its residents on a whole were considered to be "rough". A local female was quoted as saying, "Don't make me angry 'cause I came from downtown in The Borough." Most communities have their rowdy areas. A female minister from Dillon, SC schooled me on a section in her city known as "New Town" while hosting a tour for her church group on board a large motor coach: "You don't have to tell us about rough neighborhoods, some of these people are from New Town. And just because some areas are rough, it doesn't mean that all of their citizens have the same reputation." My sister-in-law Deborah is from New Town in Dillon and I've never considered her to be a rough person. On the other hand, my brother Purvis certainly deserves the "Rough Award!"

Macedonia African Methodist Episcopal Church is located at 48 Alexander St. in The Borough. Often the church's parking lot is the setting to demonstrate the *Charleston Clap* while singing *We Are Climbing Jacob's Ladder*. This three-fold clap is a traditional West African rhythm and traveled to the Caribbean and to coastal areas in the US southeast with the enslaved. When Mr. Tour Guide demonstrates the clap while leading *Jacob's Ladder*, frequently we escalate to "having church" on the tour bus.

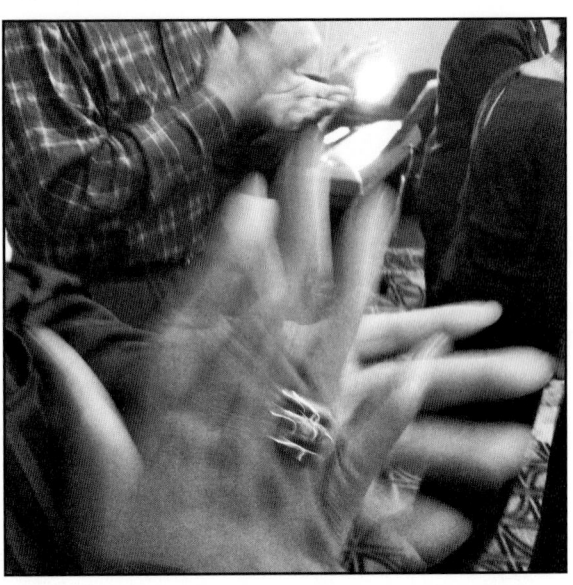

It can be tricky to get an in-focus photo of the Charleston Clap once it starts to roll. This pic is from a Feb. 2016 Choraliers Music Club of Charleston concert. I've been a performing member since 1987.

Macedonia AME has been known to have a very emotional worship service with shouting and foot stomping which tends to shock some guests. Visitors who're familiar with the Black church experience speak out: "Where we're from, the Methodists and Presbyterians are quiet and reserved, and the Baptists, Holiness and Pentecostals are noisy," one visitor mentioned. Mr. Tour Guide's response, "You are in Charleston where some Baptists are quiet, they don't shout. And the visitors continue, "Today, most churches, Black and White, are emotional more than they have ever been." Even a Jehovah's Witness agreed. In 1998, some of my tourists joined in on the singing (as some voluntarily do) and a church sister became emotional and testified, "The Bible says you are supposed to praise Him!" Her emotions almost turned out the tour! Some churchgoers have mentioned when hearing this story either, "She got happy," or "She got loose," or "She was in the Spirit," or "She got carried away." Newcomers to Charleston often request recommendations for a church service. I remember one group who had their minds set on attending another Black church, but after the singing in front

Tourists Can Say the Darndest Things!

of Macedonia and our discussion, they said, "We changed our minds about the other church; we'll worship *here* tomorrow."

A cousin, to whom I was very close, the Rev. Levern Stevenson (1932 - 2005), was the pastor of Macedonia Church for fifteen years beginning in the early 1970s. On Saturday, February 28, 2009, his son Bruce Levern Stevenson, now residing in Spotsylvania, VA, was anxious to show his wife Charlene and stepson James the church from the tour bus. On Tuesday, April 28, 2009, I had the pleasure of having the Rev. Stevenson's daughter, Michelle Stevenson, at that time residing in Alexandria, VA and now in Washington, DC, and her boyfriend Louis Harvey on the tour. Both Bruce and Michelle were proud to let it be known that they were once members of Macedonia and that their father served as one of its pastors. If Bruce and Michelle were on the tour today, they would let it be known that one of the Emanuel 9, the Rev. Clementa Pinckney, was their cousin, and they would mention the close relationship that existed between Clementa and their father. The Rev. Levern Stevenson was Clementa's great uncle and mentor (Clementa's maternal grandmother and the Rev. Stevenson were siblings.)

The back of the church where we pull over and park faces East Bay St., and as the tour bus moves away from Macedonia, visitors and locals cannot help but mention Saffron Café & Bakery located next door. The restaurant is well-known for its delicious desserts, and one can enter it from either Alexander St. or from East Bay St. Those who have weaknesses for sweets engage in sugary conversation: "Their desserts are *so* good, and the pounds just add up," confessed Mr. Preston from FL rubbing his pot belly with no shame. I'm sure Mr. Tour Guide wasn't the only one on the bus who noticed that Mr. Preston appeared to be eight months pregnant. No one bothered to ask when the baby was due though. Ellen had a message for those who have cravings for sweets and are overweight: "What's the big deal with Americans eating sweets and talking about weight? We just need to discipline ourselves and control what we put in our mouths. Fat people can have desserts."

I Remember...

In 2004, a grieving widow shared the following joke: "On this farm was a rooster, a hen, a cow, a bull and a zebra. The zebra questioned all the farm animals wanting to know what they did for the farmer. The rooster said, 'I crow and wake him up in the mornings.' The hen said, 'I give him eggs.' The cow said, 'I give him milk.' The zebra looked at the bull to respond; the bull ignored the zebra and continued eating grass. As the zebra continued to stare at the bull, demanding an answer, the bull held up his head and looked at the zebra and said, 'You know what? If I could just get those striped pajamas off of you, I will show you what I do for the farmer!'"

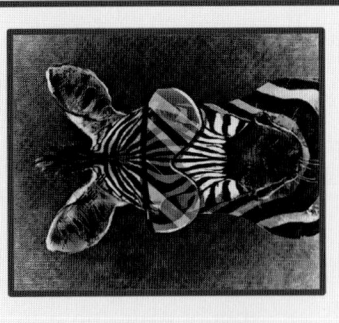

My very first step-on bus tour: These are tours conducted on chartered buses or vans, and the guide steps on board the vehicle and conducts the tour. In the Spring of 1987, Bob Small and Alada Shinault-Small, owners of Living History Tours, hired newly-licensed me to do a "step-on". Without having the experience of tour stops and controlling the group to stay together and not stray yet, as we unloaded on the corner of Broad and Church Streets to walk through the French Quarter, the group scattered and some walked several blocks to The Market to buy food! As a result, the rented bus was late getting back to the starting point, and the Smalls incurred extra cost. The group did apologize for scattering and not returning in a timely fashion. One of the ladies said, "I was just hungry and just HAD to eat!"

In 2007, while touring a small group, one woman's cell phone kept ringing, and she used it at every tour stop. Another woman, who was apparently annoyed by this, said to her, "You are truly the cell phone queen."

Blah blah blah blah. Blah blah blah?

6 | The Market

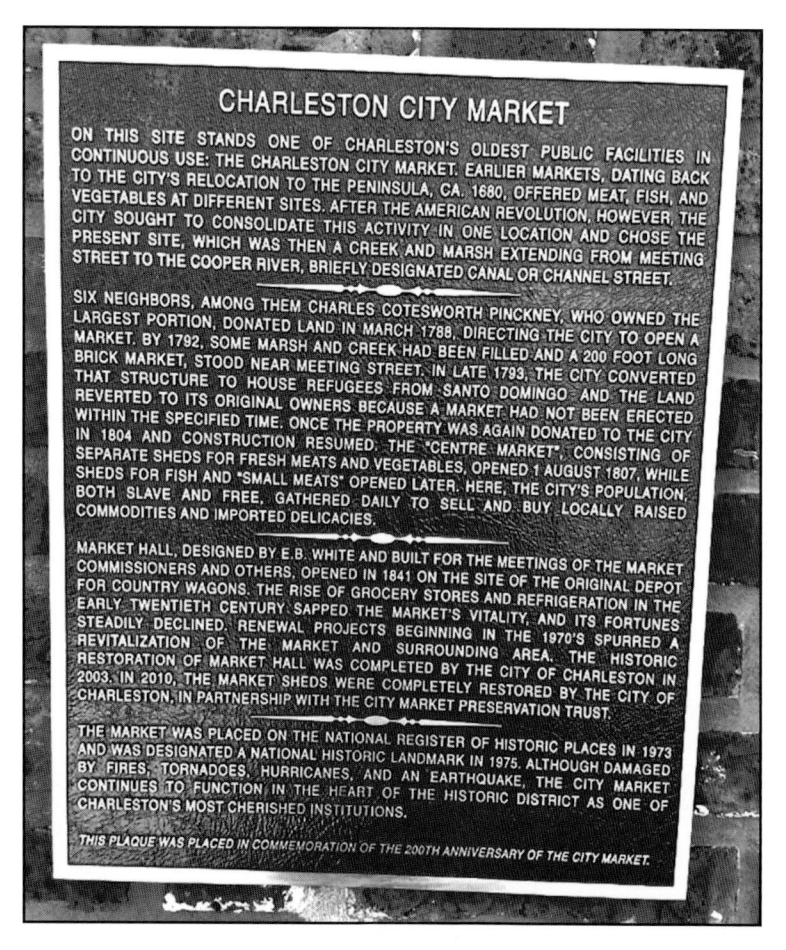

This plaque is affixed on the City Market building at the corner of Market & East Bay Sts.

The Charleston City Market sets on the site of a filled-in creek and marshy lands that were donated for a city market in 1788 with the stipulation that the property revert back to the families if used for other purposes. The Centre Market was finally completed in 1807 and extended from Meeting St. to the Cooper River. Market Hall, facing Meeting St., was built in 1841 in the Roman Revival style, so it looks like a Roman temple. Bull and sheep skulls decorate the stucco frieze, indicating that it was a meat market. The frieze is located above the columns and encircles the building. The second floor of Market Hall houses the Daughters of the Confederacy museum.

During the 1800s, butchers threw meat scraps into the streets in The Market area, and the "Charleston eagles" - buzzards - kept the area very clean. These scavengers were protected by law because of their valuable clean-up service. "One can only imagine during those days the atmosphere of the market at the end of the day with those buzzards looking forward to their daily meal," said Edward from ME. "Charleston eagles, no matter what you call those scavengers, were still buzzards," a history teacher from the Piedmont region of SC noted. Someone else said, "A buzzard is a buzzard no matter how you try to dress them up." The most popular reactions to this historical tidbit have been, "Oh how gross!", "Not a pretty scene," and "Those buzzards got the job done!" Although The Market is much too often called "The Slave Market", enslaved African Americans worked there and were sent there to shop, but were never sold there.

Until the 1970s, most of the vendors in the Market were African Americans; many were farmers from nearby areas such as James, Johns, Wadmalaw, Edisto and Yonges Islands and Mount Pleasant. Historically, African American street vendors traveled throughout The Market area enticing buyers with their rhythmic street cries. Today, the atmosphere at The Market is much different. Fresh produce, seafood and meat are no longer sold; rather, crafts, clothing, jewelry and household items dominate the vendors' wares. While the majority of the vendors today are Whites, most of the Black vendors present sell sweetgrass creations, seasonings, personal products like body oils and lotions, and decorative items.

Edna Wright Taylor and her daughter Jonzetta Taylor Goodwin are vendors at The Market and sell different types of seasonings and seasoned rice. Edna followed in her father's footsteps as a Market vendor; he remained a vendor until his death. While

Mr. Tour Guide embraces Jonzetta Taylor Goodwin at her family's stand in The Market.

strolling on Market St., both of them usually give a big wave and hello to the tour bus; and of course, Mr. Tour Guide gives them free advertisement - "When you go to The Market, please see Edna or her daughter Jonzetta if you want good seasonings for whatever dish you prepare. Take a good look at them." Folks will quickly jot down their names, and Edna and Jonzetta have always been grateful for the referred business. There are restaurants, shops, art galleries, hotels, bars, carriage tours and other businesses located in the vicinity around The Market buildings. When a cruise ship is in town and docked nearby at the SC Ports Authority terminal, the entire Market area is blanketed with even more visitors.

According to Edna Wright Taylor, five generations of the Wright family have been vendors at The City Market selling vegetables, fruit and seasonings. This legacy commenced with Edna's grandmother Lucy Wright and passed down to her father Walter Wright, Sr. (1901-1976), to her and her siblings (Dorothy, Harold, Joseph, James, Walter Jr., and Mary), to her children (Charles, Anthony and Jonzetta), and to nieces and nephews. Growing up on the peninsula on Kirkland Lane in Harleston Village, Edna also reminisced about her father and her uncle Samuel Wright selling vegetables on a wagon pulled by a mule throughout downtown streets until the 1960s. Samuel Wright, who resided on Short St., also in Harleston Village, was the last street vendor to transport produce in this manner. Edna's family has worked throughout the various buildings at The Market, but mainly in Building C, located between State and East Bay Sts. Jonzetta vividly remembers that when she was a child, there were mainly Black vendors in The Market. Edna, Jonzetta and her husband Rodney Goodwin also sell Gullah Bibles titled *De Nyew Testament,* which is *The New Testament* translated into Gullah. The English translation is included along the sides on each page for those who are not yet fluent in the Gullah language. Mr. Tour Guide often refers visitors who inquire about purchasing a Gullah Bible to these vendors.

Edna's is located in The Charleston Market in Bldg. C.

Editor's Note - While growing up on St. Philip St. in the Elliottborough section of Charleston, I can remember sitting on the front steps of our house and watching Mr. Wright come down St. Philip St. from Line St. perched at the front of his wagon which was always full of produce. He made house calls to certain families, and ours was one. Al Miller teases me because when he shared the info with me that the Wrights had told him, we realized that the Mr. Wright who I remembered regularly stopping in front of our house was the same Mr. Wright who was related to Edna and Jonzetta. I mentioned to Al about my childhood remembrance of the big horse that pulled the produce cart with Mr. Wright steering, reins in hand. I called the mule a horse, it looked like a horse to me then, and that's how I remembered it. Being raised in the city, I knew nothing about the difference between a horse and a mule. In fact, I was grown before I learned the difference. Al, on the other hand, being from a rural area has always known that difference, from childhood on up. He thinks that my calling Mr. Wright's mule a horse is the funniest thing, and still brings it up from time to time to "pick at me".

Left Walter Wright, Sr. (age 68) and grandson Anthony Taylor (age 5) are pictured in The Market, late 1960s. **Center** This photo of Edna Wright Taylor was featured in "Food & Wine" magazine in the 1980s. **Right** Jonzetta Taylor Goodwin at age 4 helping to sell produce in The Market. *Photos courtesy of Jonzetta Taylor Goodwin*

A popular venue for shoppers seeking African and African American art is Chuma Gullah Gallery, located in the Market's Great Hall. Works by renowned SC Low Country visual artist Jonathan Green are featured; his "Gullah Images" series offers glimpses of the state's coastal cultural traditions. Artwork by Columbia, SC visual artist John W. Jones is also featured at the Gallery. His "Color of Money" series piques interest when folks discover that the paintings are based on actual sketches of enslaved people found on Confederate currency. Jones' paintings highlighting Gullah Geechee and Southern history and culture are in demand also. And - Mr. Jones' depiction of aerial Charleston is showcased on the cover of this very publication.

Prior to relocating to the Great Hall in The Market, the business was called Gallery Chuma and was located at 43 John St. in a two-story building across from that side of the Visitor's Center. The name changed to Chuma Gullah Gallery after relocating to The Market. Originals, limited editions, prints and framing services were located upstairs, and the downstairs gallery featured Jonathan Green's works. Annette Green Howell, Green's sister, was employed by Gallery

Chuma from 1995-2005, and she operated the lower gallery. Being very proud of Jonathan's work, Mr. Tour Guide often told tourists who she was and made them promise never to mention the fact that she was Jonathan's sister, Annette wanted to keep her identity low-key. She knew my admiration for her brother's artwork and also knew that I was the one giving away her identity, but she wasn't upset about it. On one occasion, she mentioned the fact that a woman confronted her about being Jonathan's sister and that Al Miller mentioned it on the tour bus. Annette made her believe that I was telling a lie, and the woman said to her, "You know, these tour guides will tell you almost anything for you to believe them." We both had a good laugh when Annette shared this incident with me.

Chuma Gullah Gallery is located in the Great Hall at The Market. Al Miller & Barbara Nwokike chat at the rear of the photo. Barbara & her husband Chuma own the gallery.

Sweetgrass basket vendors are very prevalent in The Market. The utilitarian craft originated in the Old World and was brought to the southeastern US coast by enslaved West Africans who discovered what local materials that they could use to continue the tradition here. Sweetgrass, pine needles and/or bulrush are sewn in rows and stitched with palmetto strips. Today baskets are crafted mainly by women, but it's not unusual to see men making them as well. During enslavement, men made very large fanner baskets that were critical for processing rice. Baskets were also used for storing and transporting goods. This craft has been passed down from one generation to the next, and males have always been involved. Some women will tell you that male in-laws taught them how to make baskets. Regrettably, some people who are not familiar with this ancient craft allude to male basket makers as being "funny" or "gay". This explains why some males will not sew baskets publicly.

Other sweetgrass basket makers are present at the post office at the Four Corners of Law (the intersection of Broad and Meeting Sts.), at the Visitor's

Center, along Highway 17 North in Mt. Pleasant, and at various other sites throughout the Charleston area. Some visitors complain that the baskets are too expensive. After explaining the history of the baskets, the process of gathering the materials, time involved and durability, harsh thoughts are usually softened. Sometimes views change even more when the process is explained by a basket maker - hearing the story right from the horse's mouth. "Some people will complain no matter what," one basket maker said. She continued, "They don't realize that our lives are in danger when we gather up the sweetgrass in remote areas. There are times when we have to worry about wild animals, snakes and red bugs. Today the grass is not plentiful like it used to be because of development and private property; therefore, some of us have to get it from Florida."

Brenda of Morganton, NC, mentioned how much she admired a basket while shopping at the City Market. The price tag read $30 she thought, but was $300 instead. She was ready to purchase it, but after realizing that she had a missed a "0," she quickly placed it back. Everybody laughed as she shared her story on the bus. In the

Female vendors like these were commonly seen throughout Charleston up through the 20th century. They continued the Old World tradition of carrying head loads, which were often handmade baskets.

Photo from the New York Public Library Digital Collections

late 1990s, one of the sweetgrass basket makers at the Visitor's Center became very upset with a high school student who repeatedly gathered several of her friends who were all in the building and made insulting remarks about how expensive she thought that the baskets were: "Look, these baskets are too expensive! Then she picked up a number of the baskets, "Look, who's going to buy this basket? Look at the price! This basket is *too* expensive." The basket maker did not say anything to the student, but later shared the incident, "That child made me *so mad*! As she handled each basket she made insulting remarks until I could have strangled her!"

Sweetgrass basketry is the official SC handcraft. In addition to traditional baskets and those with added creative touches, shoppers can also find sweetgrass jewelry, key rings, trays and a host of other wearable art and household items, both functional and decorative.

Charleston Eagles

During the 19th century, the City Market was a favorite hangout for turkey buzzards, affectionately known locally as "Charleston Eagles". Unlike today, butchers were regular vendors in the Market, and the Eagles were their clean-up crew. In fact, they became such a regular fixture as butchers' helpers by quickly disposing of unwanted meat scraps and keeping the area tidy, the City imposed a $5 fine on anyone who killed them!

Photo from the New York Public Library Digital Collections

7 | Yep, We Have A French Quarter Too!

AFTER LEAVING THE MARKET, LET'S HEAD SOUTH ON MEETING ST. AND TAKE IN some of the French Quarter. "Why a French Quarter in Charleston, South Carolina?" visitors often ask. Well, the designation only goes back to 1973, and it was put in place to recognize Charleston's French heritage as well as to help preserve some 19th century warehouses that were up for demolition to make room for condos. The area is bordered to the south by Broad St., east by Concord St., west by King St. and north by Cumberland St. Thousands of Huguenots (Protestants) fled France in the late 1680s when Louis XIV revoked the Edict of Nantes. The edict guaranteed religious freedom and civil rights to the country's Huguenots who lived in a Catholic-dominated society. Records document that a large number of French Huguenots lived and/or worked in this part of Charles Towne. Furthermore, there was a substantial number of French Catholics who migrated to Charleston, some of whom owned property in this area as well. "The only French Quarter I knew about was in New Orleans and I be darn, Charleston has one too! You learn something new all the time," a visitor remarked one day. Today, The French Quarter offers visitors a diverse setting for restaurants, hotels, shops, bars, art galleries, attorney offices, theatres, banks, and homes with remarkable architectural features.

While going through the intersection of Cumberland St., it's a perfect time to mention that several blocks down to the left, heading east, is The Powder Magazine museum. It was built in 1713 and is the state's oldest public building, used to store the city's gunpowder during the colonial period. The tile roof is typical of the period, and the walls are 35 inches thick, almost three feet - which usually causes the folks on the bus to remark "Whoa!" or "What?!"

Beneath the triangular tile roof is a layer of bricks. The bricks cover a sand-filled attic, and the attic is above the ceiling. Also, archaeological investigations and other historical sources revealed that the building was used as a printing press and as a Madeira wine cellar during the 19th century.

The Powder Magazine museum director Alan Stello discusses 18th c. weaponry with area students.

Circular Congregational Church, 150 Meeting St. was built in 1890 and is the fourth church structure on this site. The graveyard is one of the oldest in the city. The first structure was erected on this site in 1694 and was known as the White Meeting House. This is how Meeting Street received its name, and it's one of the most traveled streets in the city, laid out around 1672. Some visitors don't pay attention to the street signs and think that guides are saying "Meating Street".

James S. Gibbes, a wealthy merchant who died in 1888, bequeathed his approximately $120,000 estate to the City of Charleston to be used for the construction or purchase of a building for an art gallery. As a result, the Beaux Arts-style Gibbes Museum of Art at 135 Meeting St., became a reality in 1905 and is known for its SC portraits and miniatures collections. The museum closed in the fall of 2014 and reopened in May 2016 after completion of a $13.5 million renovation.

The site of South Carolina Institute Hall where the Ordinance of Secession was signed on December 20, 1860 is across from the Gibbes Museum. The building seated up to 2,500 and was destroyed by the Great Fire of 1861 which also destroyed several other structures in this section of Meeting Street.

As we continue south, we approach one of the most elegant hotels in Charleston, the Mills House Hotel at 115 Meeting St. Built in 1968, this structure replaced the former hotel, but is two stories taller. The old hotel survived the

Great Fire of 1861 due to the Black staff hanging wet blankets from the windows, but causing the building to be blackened. "Look at that hotel, the gas lamps're burning, I bet the rooms are nice and cost a pretty penny," remarked Rhetta Mouzon of South NJ. Actress Elizabeth Taylor stayed at the Mills House during the filming of the movie *North and South*. It's been said that the hotel auctioned her linen, and even her handkerchief sold for $50! Some women have expressed that they think this act by the hotel was awful and gross, and the men just laugh. Bill from FL eagerly asked, "Were the linen washed?" His wife, embarrassed by his question, immediately elbowed him in the side. Everyone on the tour bus heard his question, but only a few saw him getting elbowed. Mr. Tour Guide's two cents: "I dare you to become rich and famous, someone may want your linen, underwear and the whole works." Oh, and when it becomes necessary to make a restroom stop while touring in the French Quarter, the Mills House is ideal. A gentleman who appeared to be in his late sixties or early seventies urgently exited the bus in 2008, heading quickly to the hotel. When he returned, he asked me, "Do you know the difference between a young man and an old man?" Mr. Tour Guide responded, "I'd rather you answer the question." He said, "A young man *will* piss, and an old man *must* piss; this stop was a *must* stop."

Now, if we were to park the tour bus and take in some more of the French Quarter by foot, we'll encounter some very intriguing sights. Let's walk down Chalmers Street, one of the remaining cobblestone streets and named for Dr. Lionel Chalmers, a leading physician, after he purchased property here in 1757. It extends two blocks from State St. to Meeting St. Cobblestone streets are definite attention getters. The cobblestones were used for ballast on empty cargo ships coming in from Europe to maintain the necessary weight to sail properly. When the ships loaded up goods, they no longer needed the cobblestones so locals recycled them by paving streets with them. All tour buses and carriages are prohibited from traveling on Chalmers St.

Visitors often share how they imagine the clip-clop of horse-drawn carriages on these streets back in the day, and the rough ride. And out of the mouth of babes: "What kind of street is *that?*" children regularly ask. Many visitors acknowledge having visited Savannah, GA and seeing cobblestone streets there. People of all ages agree that cobblestone streets aren't seen in most cities and are fascinated if they're not used to them. Adults verbalize about the roughness of these streets and the wear and tear that they caused on buggies and wagons during earlier days, and the auto repair bills that motorists can get if they're in a hurry and ride over them too fast today. Women have gone a step further, visualizing being pregnant and driving hurriedly down Chalmers St. - the baby might come sooner than expected. And another conversation piece is the challenge of walking on the cobblestones in high heels.

While crossing the intersection of Chalmers and Church Sts., the famous Dock Street Theatre at 135 Church St. is visible while looking over one's left shoulder. James Kress from VT pointed at the building and said in amazement, "Just *look* at that façade!" Inserted in the lobby of the old Planter's Hotel during a WPA project in the 1930s, the theatre was named after the original Dock Street Theatre which faced Queen Street (originally named Dock Street) around 1735. That 18th century building is said to have been the first one in America constructed specifically for theatrical performances. The new Dock Street Theatre opened in 1937. The City of Charleston owns the theatre, and it's been a salvation through the years to visitors for its restrooms and air conditioning. Plus, it's always refreshing to peek in on a rehearsal for an upcoming performance.

The French Huguenot Church, directly across the street from the theatre, was erected in 1844-45, and was known during the 19th century as the "tides church". According to tradition, services were timed to the tides to accommodate members arriving from and departing to nearby plantations across the Cooper River by boat. Numerous visitors misunderstand this statement, thinking guides are saying "tithes church". "We hope that church members paid their tithes back then *and* pay them today," a visitor commented.

St. Philip's Episcopal Church at 146 Church St. is further down and on the same side of the street as the Huguenot Church. Organized in 1681, it has the oldest congregation in the city. This elegant, vibrant, mesmerizing structure, rebuilt in 1838, juts out almost into the middle of Church St. and that captivates visitors. This is the second structure to be built on this site. Well-known persons such as John C. Calhoun are buried in the churchyard. Visitors love the story of John C. Calhoun's remains being moved more than once in the churchyard. A native of Abbeville Co., SC, he was a US Senator and was Vice President under John Quincy Adams and Andrew Jackson. Many know of him because of his pro-slavery views. When he died in 1850, he was buried behind St. Philip's Church. By the way, the statue of him in Marion Square, close to the Visitor Center, is facing south and its back is turned on the north. When the Civil War erupted, his remains were moved to an unmarked grave, Confederates were afraid of Union soldiers tampering with them. After the war, his remains were moved across Church St. to St. Philip's non-members graveyard. I don't anticipate his remains being moved again. Other famous persons buried in the churchyard, which is divided into an eastern and a western section, are Edward Rutledge, signer of the Declaration of Independence and a SC governor; Dubose Heyward, author of the novel *Porgy* and co-author of the opera *Porgy and Bess*; and several colonial governors and Episcopal bishops. "My husband and I worshipped there (St. Philip's) on our last trip to Charleston, and the music was *just fabulous!*" Mrs. Stockton from Fort Wayne, IN exclaimed with much excitement. "We heard about that John C. Calhoun guy on another tour, and who in the world would want dead bones?" Mrs. White from Bristol, TN asked. Ms. Susan from Laurens, SC put in her two cents with a distinct southern accent: "I reckon he was for the southern cause so they had to protect him from those Yankee soldiers. I guess it *was* a little silly to move him so many times."

The Old Slave Mart Museum at 6 Chalmers St. is coming up on the left. It has exhibits and interactive stations in which visitors can get a true sense of the realities of American enslavement while physically being present in a space where people of African descent were shuttled to, inspected, bid on, became the personal property of whomever bid the highest amount of money, and then whisked away - with or without the family members with whom they came there.

Slave auctions were commonly held outside in this section of Charleston. This area was bursting with commercial activity during the 18th and 19th centuries just like it is today. The area just north of the Old Exchange and Provost Dungeon on East Bay St. at Broad St. was a regular site for auctioning Africans and African Americans. However, a July 1856 city ordinance prohibited the further practice of these outdoor sales events. Ryan's Mart at 6 Chalmers St. opened the very same day that the ordinance went into effect, continuing the profit-driven business activity, but indoors. The property was a complex of buildings that extended from Chalmers St. back to Queen St., the next parallel street to the north. The complex consisted of a yard enclosed by a brick wall and three buildings - one was a four-story brick double tenement that faced Queen St. partially containing a barracoon, a Portuguese word meaning slave jail. It's said that it was also called "the nigger jail". The other two buildings were a kitchen and a "dead house" (morgue). The last slave auctions in this building were held in November 1863 when the owners, Thomas Ryan and Z.B. Oakes, left to fight in the Civil War.

The Old Slave Mart Museum, owned and operated by the City of Charleston, is the former site of Ryan's Mart where countless enslaved African Americans were sold at public auctions from 1856-1863.

Charles Carleton Coffin was a reporter with the *Boston Journal*. He visited Charleston in early 1865 when he was about age forty-one. As he walked the streets of the war-torn and empty city, he recorded his observations and published them along with what he witnessed throughout much of the post-Civil War South. This is what he encountered at 6 Chalmers St.:

> *Amid these surroundings was the Slave-Mart, — a building with a large iron gate in front, above which, in large gilt letters, was the word MART. The outer iron gate opened into a hall about sixty feet long by twenty broad, flanked on one side by a long table running the entire length of the hall, and on the other by benches. At the farther end a door, opening through a brick wall, gave entrance to a yard. The door was locked. I tried my bootheel, but it would not yield. I called a freedman to my aid. Unitedly we took up a great stone, and gave a blow. Another, and the door of the Bastile went into splinters. Across the yard was a four-story brick building, with grated windows and iron doors, — a prison. The yard was walled by high buildings. He who entered there left all hope behind. A small room adjoining the hall was the place where women were subjected to the lascivious gaze of brutal men. There were the steps, up which thousands of men, women, and children had walked to their places on the table, to be knocked off to the highest bidder.*

From 1878-1937 a tenement for African Americans and an auto repair shop were located at 6 Chalmers. From 1938-1964 Miriam B. Wilson started a museum highlighting African and African American visual arts and craftsmanship. Two sisters, Judith Wragg Chase and Louise Wragg Graves, took the business over in 1964 and operated it until 1987. The City of Charleston bought the building in 1988 and reopened it to the public as a museum in the fall of 2007.

The next three pages are a slave sale broadside. It's an example of the flyers that circulated regularly to announce auctions, to include having a detailed listing of the enslaved men, women, children and infants that were available to purchase along with a mention of their ages, skills and any other info that was considered relevant. I'll share some thoughts afterwards.

LIST OF

A PRIME AND ORDERLY GANG OF

47 NEGROES,

Accustomed to the Culture of Long Cotton and Provisions,

IN CHRIST CHURCH PARISH; BY

P. J. PORCHER & BAYA

On FRIDAY, the 21st of January, '59,

AT 10 O'CLOCK, A. M. WILL BE SOLD AT

RYAN'S MART, Chalmers-st.

IN THE

CITY OF CHARLESTON,

A REMARKABLY PRIME AND ORDERLY GANG OF

FORTY-SEVEN NEGROES

Accustomed to the culture of Long Cotton and Provisions, in Christ Church Parish.

AMONG WHICH ARE

THREE VALUABLE CARPENTERS, AN EXPERIENCED DRIVER,

AND A FIRST RATE COACHMAN.

CONDITIONS OF SALE—One-third Cash; Balance in one and two years, secured by bond, mortgage, and approved personal security, with interest from day of sale, payable annually. Purchasers to pay P. J. P. & B. for papers.

	No.	NAMES.	Age.	QUALIFICATIONS.
	1	Simon,	55	Carpenter.
	2	Stephen,	45	Experienced driver.
	3	Lydia,	32	Field hand.
	4	Celia,	16	" "
	5	Simon,	14	" " and Cart-boy.
	6	Martha,	8	
	7	Rachael,	5	
510 8	8	Doll,	42	Field hand, dairy maid and midwife
	9	Sam,	30	Field hand.
	10	Tenah,	30	" "
610	11	Alex,	16	" "
	12	Sophy,	14	" "
	13	Eliza,	12	
	14	Julia,	4	
	15	Phillis,	20	Prime Field hand.
	16	John,	4	
died 9	17	Infant.		
(Withdrawn)	18	Lizzy,	25	Field hand.
	19	Primus,	12	
	20	Frank,	6	
	21	Scipio,	3	
5	22	Pompey,	6 mo.	
115 1	23	Charlotte,	55	Nurse.
	24	Jerry,	30	Prime field hand and jobbing carpenter.
975 2	25	Amelia,	28	Prime field hand.
780	26	Toney,	35	Prime field hand.
2	27	Nanny,	35	" "
600	28	Andrew,	45	Good carpenter.
2	29	Beckey,	40	Field hand.
550 1	30	Lide,	35	Coachman and hostler.

	No.	NAMES.	Age.	QUALIFICATIONS.
370		31	Julia,	45	Field hand and poultry minder.
	2	32	Gabriel,	9	
		33	Pompey,	45	Field hand.
		34	Rinah,	28	" "
		35	Isaac,	7	
515		36	Nancy,	4	
	5	37	Infant,	6 mo.	
600	1	38	Abel,	19	Prime.
		39	Joanna,	50	Field hand and gardener.
		40	Elsey,	35	" "
560		41	Major,	21	" "
	4	42	Infant	4 mo.	
		43	Ned,	40	Prime field hand.
340	2	44	Willoughby,	40	One-half hand.
		45	Grace,	28	Prime.
350		46	Nelson,	2	
	3	47	Infant.		

The previous three pages are from the Hutson Lee Papers (Collection 1058.00, Folder 11/260/1) at the South Carolina Historical Society.

Page 1:

- Christ Church Parish is listed twice. It was a portion of present-day Mount Pleasant, east of Charleston across the Cooper River, and is one of many examples of South Carolina's historical and cultural ties to Barbados. This parish's name is the same as one of the eleven parishes there.
- Look at the sales terms. Now you know why it's been discovered that some of today's well-known banks that have acquired other banks through the years ended up having a history of being owners of people held in bondage. For example, if a planter took out a bank loan to satisfy the one-third cash down requirement and then defaulted, those humans became the bank's "property". Check out these websites: http://money.cnn.com/2005/06/02/news/fortune500/wachovia_slavery/ and https://www.theguardian.com/world/2005/jan/22/usa.davidteather
- Notice the variety of fonts that are used. It's interesting that 19th century printers had that many choices, which they obviously put to use to draw attention to the info.

Page 2:

- The handwritten numbers on the left are perhaps the preferred minimum bids.
- The people's names show mostly the Americanized identities that they were forced to take in the overall attempt to erase any and all West African traditions.
- Their variety of high end skills that were bragged on included on the broadside prove that the success and prosperity that the buyers, sellers and brokers *and* their descendants achieved were a result of West Africans' forced migration and forced servitude.
- Amelia, age 28 and listed as #25, was a "Prime field hand" in the cotton industry, a major cash crop. 975 is written in the margin by her name, probably meaning that the seller desired a minimum bid of $975.00. Nine-hundred seventy-five dollars in 1859 would've been worth approximately $28,700 in 2015.

The Great Earthquake of 1886

On Tuesday, August 31, 1886 at approximately 9:50 pm, Charleston and surrounding areas experienced a catastrophic earthquake, later estimated at between 6.9 - 7.3 on the Richter Scale.

The Richter Scale was developed in 1935 by Ohio-born seismologist Charles F. Richter to measure earthquake magnitude.

Tremors were felt from Cuba to New York, Bermuda to the Mississippi River; & cities in Alabama, Ohio and Kentucky sustained structural damage.

In the Charleston area about 100 people died, and there were 8 million dollars in damages in 1886 currency. Countless brick buildings were repaired with earthquake bolts inserted in them to pull the buildings back together. The plates are in various sizes & shapes, but round ones are most common. On the right is an earthquake bolt with an X-shaped plate.

Hibernian Hall at 105 Meeting St. was one of many structures to sustain devastating damage from the earthquake, see below left. It was built in 1840 to house the Hibernian Society, an Irish benevolent organization founded in 1801. See the Hall as it looks now below right. *1886 photo from the The Charleston Museum*

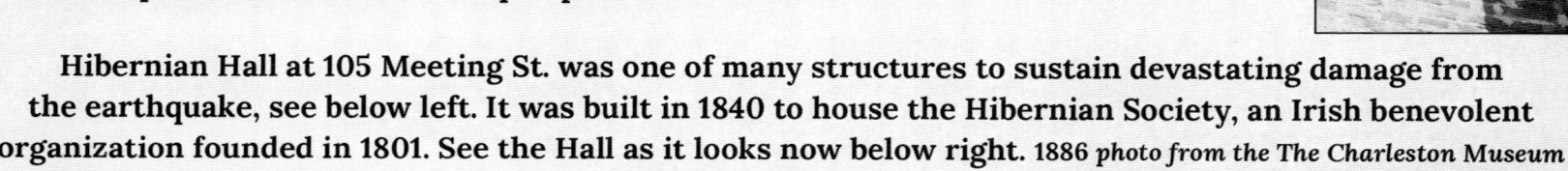

8 | Broad Street, South of Broad & The Battery

CHARLES TOWNE WAS ESTABLISHED IN 1670 AFTER VERY ROUGH BEGINNINGS FOR the three-ship expedition that departed London in August 1669. After a series of hurricanes, equipment failures and other delays, only one ship, the *Carolina*, left Bermuda in February 1670 for Port Royal in present-day Beaufort County, SC. By the middle of March, the group reached Bull Island, located near Mt. Pleasant, in present-day Charleston County - quite a distance from their intended destination.

The head of the Kiawah Native American nation, who was considered to be a friend of the English, took the travelers down to Port Royal, but encouraged them to settle on high ground on the banks of what's known today as the Ashley River where the soil was decent and where they would be safer from Spanish Floridians and unfriendly natives. The Kiawah leader, called a Cacique, probably launched into survival mode thinking that if the English did colonize where he suggested, they would protect him and his people from their enemy the Westoes - other natives, and they could gain access to the newcomers' firearms. So in April 1670, the approximately 120 settlers made their home at the mouth of the river Kiawah. The river was later renamed Ashley after Lord Anthony Ashley Cooper, Earl of Shaftesbury, one of the eight Lords Proprietors - loyal and devoted supporters of the English king Charles II.

Six weeks later, the sloop *Three Brothers* arrived after heading for Port Royal and getting off course also. It was a replacement vessel for one of the initial two ships that encountered major problems. Instead, the passengers ended up as far south as Georgia, ran into tremendous hardship, to include losing a number of passengers, then turned north. Thanks to some area natives, they were reunited with their fellow travelers. The transplants named their location Albermarle Point after George Monck, Duke of Albermarle, another one of the Lords Proprietors.

There was a family of African descent among those first settlers - John, Elizabeth and John, Jr. who were enslaved. The town was eventually named Charles Towne after King Charles II. That area is currently a 664-acre state park named Charles Towne Landing and is famous for being South Carolina's birthplace and the first permanent English settlement south of Virginia.

Around 1680, the Charles Towne residents relocated about five miles away to the southern end of the peninsula that was across the Ashley River, an area that they had surveyed some years earlier and had named Oyster Point (it's said that they discovered a huge amount of oyster shells there.) This land mass was located at the junction of the Ashley and another river, the Cooper. It too was renamed after the Shaftesbury earl. The previous village became known as Old Towne. The Lords Proprietors dictated that the new town be laid out with straight streets, large blocks and a central public square. The town developed quickly with houses, churches and small farms. Walled fortifications enclosed a large portion of the town to prevent attacks from both the river and land sides. As a result, Charleston was one of three walled cities in North America and the only English one. The other two were in the French Canadian province Quebec and Spanish St. Augustine, FL.

Now, let's explore this older portion of the peninsula which would have been within the safety net of the wall. Charles Towne became Charleston, by the way, in 1783 when the city was incorporated. Starting from the east end of Broad St. at the corner of East Bay St., one cannot help but notice the Old Exchange and Provost Dungeon. Built in 1771 on the site of the 17th century police station called the "Court of Guard", a 1965 excavation resulted in the discovery of a curved portion of the original wall documented on a 1711 map as a battery called "The Half Moon". This is the only section of the original wall that's visible to the public.

Old Exchange staff that are dressed in colonial outfits are usually on the porch waving at passersby. The building was constructed to serve as a Custom House (Exchange), and also served as a post office during the 19th century. The Great Hall on the top floor was used for some political gatherings, and when President George Washington visited Charleston in 1791, he was entertained there at a fancy ball held in his honor.

Working our way west, on the northeast corner of Broad and Church Sts is a tour bus stop for loading and unloading chartered buses. The City restricts large bus travel to certain streets, as well as designating specific spots to park and load/unload (with time limits). So, in order to visit sites like Catfish Row, the Heyward-Washington House, the Dock Street Theatre, the Old Slave Mart Museum and others, we have to unload within fifteen minutes then walk to these sites. Many folks who have medical conditions, are handicapped and who don't desire to walk usually remain on the bus. If it's a typical 90+ degrees summer day with high humidity, some will definitely remain on the bus. If it's raining, women

Tourists Can Say the Darndest Things!

The Old Exchange Building is considered to be one of the three most historically significant colonial buildings in the US along with Town Hall in Philadelphia & Faneuil Hall in Boston.

"Captain Sean Wallis" is one of the Old Exchange's interpreters who shares its history with visitors.

especially will remain on the bus to avoid getting their hair wet. One rainy day, Doris from Winter Haven, FL asked, "Mr. Miller, if I get off in the rain will you pick up the tab for a new hair do?" Mr. Tour Guide replied, "Taking care of a new do is *not* a part of the tour package."

"The corner of hell and confusion" is what some in the industry call that particular intersection. Tempers flare when chartered bus drivers are not back in time to load up, especially when it's hot, cold or rainy. One driver decided after a group drop-off to get a quick snack, turned off the engine then the bus wouldn't start back up. Other drivers have gotten lost, not being familiar with Charleston streets. Others don't study the City's map for bus drivers and don't believe us when we tell them that their GPSs may steer them wrong.

It's amazing to see the number of middle and high school students who drag and walk so slowly when we disembark at Broad and Church Sts. to walk to various sites. "Walk faster, you walk as if you're senior citizens. We have a tight schedule," Mr. Tour Guide has to announce. A chaperon followed up once with, "They are lazy and don't exercise. They eat at every opportunity and spend too much time in front of the television and computer."

The site of Shepheard's Tavern, 46 Broad Street is one of the first buildings that one notices at the Broad and Church Sts. northeast corner. Known at various times also as The Corner Tavern, The City Tavern and Swallow's Tavern, many historical events took place at that location: One of the first Masonic lodges in the US was organized there on October 29, 1736 as Solomon's Lodge No. 1, Free and Accepted Masons; the first Chamber of Commerce in America was organized there in 1773; the first Scottish Rite lodge, the Supreme Council, 33rd Degree, Ancient and Accepted Scottish Rite of Free Masonry was organized there in 1801; the first record of a theatrical season in Charleston was performed in its long room which was called the Courtroom because it was rented out for court meetings. A city post office was once there, and it was used for events and meetings. As you can see, Charleston taverns had much more going on in them than drinking and eating. The building was demolished in 1928 to construct the present bank building, built for $280,000. "Just imagine if these old buildings and the dirt could talk, oh what stories would be told!" one visitor remarked. In addition, there are lots of carriage tours in this vicinity. "Oh look at the horses!" children repeat again and again with excitement. And adults make the corrections, "Those aren't all horses, some are mules." And if the animals have to relieve themselves with a number 1 and/or number 2, children really go wild!

The Charleston branch of the Freedman's Bank, a national bank for African Americans, was located at 58 Broad St. from 1869-1874 and located to the west of the former tavern building. The branch had 5,500 depositors and about $350,000 in deposits in 1873. Mismanagement at other branches and manipulation by White NY financiers caused the bank to fail in 1874.

The upcoming intersection is the infamous Four Corners of Law at Broad and Meeting Sts. Robert Ripley, the founder of *Believe It Or Not*, labeled the intersection in this way. This corner was set aside as a Civic Square in the Grand Modell, the 17th century plan of the City, to be used for public structures, and that has always been the case. Each building on each corner represents a type of a law: On the southeast corner, St. Michael's Protestant Episcopal Church represents God's law; the Post Office and Federal Courthouse on the southwest corner represents federal law; City Hall on the northeast corner represents municipal or city Law and the County Courthouse on the northwest corner represents county law. Charleston is said to be the only city in the world to have a Four Corners of Law. Mr. Tour Guide informs everyone on the bus that at one time, a couple could complete four acts on this corner: marry in the church, pick up mail at the post office, pay taxes at City Hall and file for the divorce at the courthouse. This was a one-stop-shop corner. An elderly gentleman from the Midwest set the record straight by saying, "Young man, a couple could do more than that on this corner. Well, they may get into an argument as to who is going to pay the taxes, one may kill the other and the funeral will be held in the church and the trial at the courthouse." Ollie Prince from GA said, "And in my city, you can obtain the death certificate from the courthouse."

St. Michael's Episcopal Church at 71 Meeting St. was built in 1761, and is the oldest church edifice on the peninsula; it's on the site of the first Anglican church built south of VA. The clock and bells were imported from England in 1764, and the bells were sent back to England several times for repairs and recasting. During the Revolutionary War, the bells were taken back to England as a war prize. They ring each quarter of the hour. President George Washington worshipped in pew number forty-three during his 1791 Southern Tour, and so did Confederate General Robert E. Lee seventy years later in 1861. The 186-ft. steeple was painted black during the Civil War to ensure that it was less of an easy target for Federal shells, and it was used as a fire lookout and alarm tower until the late 19th century. Due to the 1886 earthquake, the entire steeple sank eight inches. John Rutledge and Charles Cotesworth Pinckney, signers of the US Constitution, are a couple of the famous persons buried in the churchyard. St. Michael's bells appear to chime at the most perfect time while the church is being talked about, as if they were answering in return, "I hear you talking about me, now listen to me chime." This occurrence is even more effective on a walking tour when the visitors look up toward the steeple and the bells respond. On tour buses, one can hear the chimes, but it may be difficult for some to see the steeple. In the movie *North and South*, Madeline said, "I hear the bells of St. Michael's, I must go now."

The US Post Office and Courthouse at 83 Broad St. is the more modern of the buildings at the Four Corners of Law. Built in 1896, the post office occupies the first floor, and the courtroom is on the second floor. Originally, a mid 18th century Guardhouse (police station) stood on that spot, the 1886 earthquake demolished it.

The Charleston County Courthouse at 84 Broad St. was built in 1792 in the neoclassical architectural style. The SC State House was constructed on this site in 1753 because initially Charleston was the state capital. In 1786, the Assembly voted to move the capital to Columbia, a more centralized location. Fire destroyed the statehouse building in 1788 while the second state house was being built in Columbia.

City Hall at 80 Meeting St. was built in 1801 in the Adamesque style by Gabriel Manigault, known as the "Gentleman Architect", who studied in Europe and designed his brother's house, the Joseph Manigault House at 350 Meeting Street, across from the Visitor Center. The building was first constructed as the First Bank of the United States. The bank's charter was lost in 1811, and the building became City Hall in 1818. Prior to the bank, the public beef market was located on the site.

The old beef market stood precisely where the City hall now is. It was a neat building, supported by brick arches, and surmounted by a belfry. This I saw

burnt down in the great fire of June, 1796.... It commenced in the afternoon in Lodge alley near the Bay, somewhere to the east or northeast of St. Philip's Church, from which quarter the wind blew. In its progress it would have destroyed that venerable building but for the heroic intrepidity of a negro, who, at the risk of his life, climbed to the very summit of the belfry, and tore off the burning shingles. It burnt the original French church, where the Huguenot refugees had worshipped for upwards of a century previous to that time.
– From Charles Fraser's *Reminiscences of Charleston*, 1854

The "negro" who displayed "heroic intrepidity", by the way, was an enslaved boatman. He was released from bondage for saving the church.

If we were to turn around and head east, we'd pass by the site of the Jones Hotel on the right, and the info that I share about it always gets attention. Jehu Jones was born enslaved in 1769. He bought his freedom in 1798 then launched a successful tailoring business that allowed him to branch off into real estate in Charleston and on nearby Sullivan's Island. Nine years after he became a free man he bought enslaved African Americans to assist him with his businesses. In 1809, the entrepreneur bought a house and lot on Broad St. behind St. Michael's Church for $2000 and converted the house into a hotel. In 1815, he bought a 1774 three and one-half story mansion and its two outbuildings next door for $13,000 and sold the other property to St. Michael's in 1816. Afterward, church officials demolished the former hotel, enabling them to extend their Meeting St. cemetery over to Broad St.

Jones abandoned his tailoring business and let his son Jehu Jr. run it. Jones Sr. and his wife Abigail then turned their full attentions to innkeeping. Their very popular exclusive hotel was known as the Jones Hotel, and it remained open until Jehu Jones' death in 1833. The complex included a two-story, six-room house and a four-room cottage along with the main building. The Jones' elite White clientele regularly praised them for the comfortable accommodations and great food.

I mentioned in Chapter Two that after Denmark Vesey's plan to free the Charleston area's enslaved population failed, the General Assembly passed acts to tighten control on free Blacks. The Joneses were among the large number of

The Jones Hotel
Sketch courtesy of The South Carolina Department of Archives and History

folks in Charleston's free Black community who were affected. The 1822 legislation required that all free males of color ages fifteen and up have a guardian. Jehu Sr. came under the guardianship of Governor John L. Wilson. Then in 1823, an act was passed that forbade any free Black person who left SC from returning. Jehu Jr., who converted from being Episcopalian to a Lutheran, was encouraged in 1832 by his pastor at St. John's Lutheran Church to travel to NY to be ordained as a missionary to Liberia to assist the freedmen there. Jones Jr. was in his forties. When he returned to Charleston, he was jailed for breaking that 1823 law. After he was released, he relocated to Philadelphia and became very active in the Lutheran Church there as a minister and a human rights advocate. Meanwhile, Jehu Jr.'s mother Abigail, her grandchildren and her daughter Ann Deas - his half-sister - had gone to NY before the acts were passed. As a result of the 1823 act, they couldn't return to Charleston. Jones Sr. then had to petition the court through his guardian to get permission to travel out of state to visit his family and to be able to return to SC. Some sources say that he made two trips, one to NY and one to FL.

Abigail Jones died before her husband, she had become an innkeeper while in NY. Jehu Sr. died in 1833 in Charleston and left an estate estimated to be worth $40,000 to his three sons and to Ann, his step-daughter. Ann, who was her stepfather's personal representative, returned to Charleston. She was required to get a pardon from the governor for re-entering the state without permission. Ann bought the Jones Hotel from the estate along with Eliza Johnson, also a free Black woman, and they operated it as Jones' Establishment from 1834 or 1835-1847. In 1852, a hotel called the Mansion House operated out of the structure. After the Civil War, the building declined to a boarding house. In 1928 a buyer planned to rebuild it on the Ashley River, so the house was dismantled. However, due to the Depression, the sections remained in storage for almost thirty years. In 1959, the former hotel's drawing room was installed in the Winterthur Museum in Winterthur, DE. A two story masonry building was constructed on the site in 1930 and housed an insurance company with a real estate component for a number of generations.

Let's turn right onto the other side of Church St., across from "the corner of hell and confusion", and head south. South of Broad or Below Broad, as many of the locals still refer to it, extends south of Broad Street to The Battery, the peninsula's southernmost point. You won't find the name written on the street signs above the street names like you commonly see in many of the other older neighborhoods though. This neighborhood is also called SOB locally. It's been said over and over and over that this area is where the s.o.b.'s live; naturally some find this statement to be very humorous, while some of the locals do not find it amusing at all. "This is where the snobs live. We heard this on other tours," a visitor once uttered with a smirk. Since 2009, many visitors are reminded of the late Pat Conroy's book *South of Broad*. Be aware that a number of the South of Broad neighborhoods that are now gorgeous examples of well-preserved historical structures that are prime real estate were not always in that condition, from the 1920s to about the 1960s much of the area was depressed.

Also be aware that many of Charleston's older neighborhoods were ethnically diverse during various time periods, and the South of Broad neighborhood was no exception. Today, most African Americans who live on the peninsula are located north of Calhoun St., and in recent years, living on the peninsula has become unaffordable for many, across ethnic lines. Factors that have caused population shifts city-wide include gentrification, eminent domain situations and homeowners choosing to sell then relocating off the peninsula.

Catfish Row at 89-91 Church St. was built about 1783 and is a three-story double tenement trimmed in red. Originally it was called Cabbage Row because in the 1920s, Black tenants planted cabbages in the courtyard and displayed them on the window sills for sale. It became known as Catfish Row due to DuBose Heyward's 1925 novel, *Porgy*, and later his and the Gershwin brothers' 1935 opera *Porgy and Bess*. The sign that reads "Catfish Row" is visible near the center arch, and the archway leads into the back courtyard with a tenant building on each side. Catfish Row was the setting for both the book and the well-known opera, but was placed on East Bay St. for literary purposes, creating a nearby river setting. Most of the African American men who actually rented here during the 1920s were fishermen and were members of the Mosquito Fleet, so called because at a distance their small boats with homemade sails looked like mosquitoes it was said.

The Heyward-Washington House at 87 Church Street is next door to Catfish Row. Built about 1771, it was the home of Thomas Heyward, the

The Heyward-Washington House is seen on the left, presently a house museum, and Catfish Row is on the right.

great-great-great grandfather of DuBose Heyward, *Porgy*'s author. Thomas Heyward was also one the state's four signers of the Declaration of Independence. President George Washington stayed here for a week during his 1791 Southern tour, and his name was added to the house's name. The house is presently a museum owned and operated by the Charleston Museum. House museum visitors are usually anxious to know in which room did Washington stay. "George Washington slept in many places," is the more popular answer that guides give.

Edwin Dubose Heyward was born in Charleston exactly a year before the 1886 earthquake and lived in a c.1785 two-story row house at 76 Church St. that's cater-cornered from "Catfish Row" and the Heyward-Washington House. When you think about how close his house was to the Cabbage Row apartments, you can imagine him relaxing outside or sitting in the window and soaking in all of the activity on the street as African American residents came, went, interacted and conducted business within eye and ear shot. His observations became a key factor in creating the characters and the activity that were a vital part of his novel *Porgy* and later *Porgy and Bess* the opera.

First Baptist Church, 61 Church Street and founded 1682, is the oldest Baptist church in the South, known as the "Mother Church of Southern Baptists." A group of Anabaptists came to Charleston from Kittery, ME to escape religious persecution. The present structure, completed in 1822, was designed by architect Robert Mills (designer of the Washington Monument and various Charleston structures). One of its pastors, the Rev. Richard Furman, was the founder of Furman University in Greenville, SC, the oldest Baptist college in the South. At the end of each school day around 3 pm, visitors wonder why there's a line of cars on Church St. and on Meeting Street. First Baptist School is ending its day, and parents are there to pick up their children. Mr. Tour Guide apologizes for the delay and almost always gets a response like, "Not a problem, we're on vacation," or "We're retired and have no babies to go home to!"

As we turn onto Water St., visitors are intrigued to know that it was originally known

Edwin Dubose Heyward lived cater-cornered from Cabbage Row, the multi-family dwelling that inspired "Catfish Row", the main setting in *Porgy & Porgy and Bess*. His house is pictured to the immediate right of the trees. The SC Legislature designated *Porgy and Bess* as the official state opera in 2001.

as Vanderhorst Creek, the waterway in which William, Lord Campbell, the last Royal Governor of SC escaped from the city during the American Revolution. This is a prime example of filled-in land. When we turn onto King St., quite a few visitors have mentioned that this section reminds them of the Georgetown section in Washington, DC because of the architecture and the closeness of the houses. However, a real estate agent who owned property in Georgetown remarked upon hearing about the constant comparison, "People *do not* know what they're talking about; this neighborhood looks nothing like Georgetown! I've said it, and you are welcome to quote me in your book." Visitors have compared this area to Annapolis, MD, Old Alexandria, VA and Philadelphia, PA as well.

The ironwork in front of the Miles Brewton House at 27 King St. is said to have been installed in response to the Denmark Vesey slave insurrection plot in 1822.

The Miles Brewton House at 27 King St. is an attention-getter as we head south toward The Battery. This house, built around 1769, is considered to be one of the finest Georgian Palladian-style houses in America. Miles Brewton, who became very wealthy buying and selling enslaved people, only enjoyed his home for ten years; in 1775 he and his family were lost at sea. His sister Rebecca Brewton Motte inherited the house. The spiked ironwork in front, called "chevaux-de-frise", is believed to have been added in 1822 after the Denmark Vesey insurrection plot. Since Whites were outnumbered by Blacks, when the news leaked out about Vesey's plan, they were petrified that the freedom-seeking enslaved people would break into their homes and attack them. Here are some of the shocking and disturbing observations made about these spikes: "There is no way anybody can crawl over that fence and not get injured." "Horrible!" "Looks like barb wire." "Ugly." "Vicious." "Frightening!" "Their ADT system back then." "Those White folks were seriously scared." In the summer of 2004, an elderly Black woman from Washington, DC commented when seeing this spiked ironwork, "They need to bring this kind of thing to Washington, DC." When I've mentioned her remark, the most popular response other than laughter has been, "She must live in Southeast." And some Washingtonians on board have quickly replied defensively, "Watch it - I live in Southeast."

The Miles Brewton House is beautiful, but the ironwork gets the focused attention. Further, inquiries have been made about whether or not the late Philip Simmons forged these spikes. Mr. Tour Guide's response: "You became so excited over the ironwork until you didn't listen or forgot what I said earlier about Mr. Simmons. He's in his nineties, this ironwork was added in 1822 - many years before Mr. Simmons was born." In April 2007, Mr. Tour Guide said, "Look to the right and take note of the Miles Brewton House." Elizabeth of Huntersville, NC immediately interjected, "Or you may look to your left and see the tattoo on this woman's hiny," meaning her butt.

After a few seconds of regaining composure, Mr. Tour Guide changed the mood of the tour by pointing out the elaborate, gorgeous Patrick O'Donnell House, 21 King Street. O'Donnell, a building contractor, built his "Italian palace" from 1852-1870. Tradition says that he built it for his bride. Because he took so long to finish it, she changed her mind and married another man. "Look at the door, the detail work, three porches - also called piazzas - one on each floor; and the carriage house with the mahogany doors!" I point out. "Had Mr. O'Donnell played his cards right, his bride-to-be would have had the house," snickered Ronald Alexander from Los Angeles, CA. Another comment: "Maybe and maybe not; the house and money aren't everything. Then again, she could have married a man with a much larger house." Cora Beckett from Bowie, MD looked at her girlfriend seated next to her and said, "Girrrl, I think I would've waited, what about you?" And one young man, a part of a youth group, remarked, "That woman was messed up; I would've taken her to see Jerry Springer!" And only a man would say, "That's just like a woman to change her mind." When this house was for sale in 2005, one woman said, "The house is gorgeous, trimmed in gold. I need an available *straight man* to *buy me* that house!" In May 2007, a Jamaican man said, "I guess that woman thought she was going to die before the house was built." Another man said, "Nooo, she was a fool!" I couldn't resist following up with, "Dah gal been fool enny?" - Gullah for "That woman was foolish, wasn't she?"

Of course everybody on the bus in 2005 wanted to know the asking price after seeing the "For Sale" sign. I informed them that it was first listed for $5.5 million and later decreased to $4.9 million. Then in 2007, I heard that it was quoted in the local newspaper that it sold for a whopping $7.2 million. In the spring of 2008, I heard that it was on the market again for 7.8 million. Betty McClain from NJ, very sophisticated in her demeanor and attire announced, "I'll search for a nice gentleman, straight of course, to purchase this grand piece of real estate for me."

In October 2008, Jasper of Winston-Salem, NC said of Mr. O'Donnell, "He should have pissed on his bride-to-be's belongings, and she would have married *him* instead of another." Where is Mr. Tour Guide going with this mention? Jasper had heard earlier on the tour the story of men who take women on dates, then ask the desired women afterwards to join them in holy matrimony. These men would then urinate on the women's belongings - hats, pocketbooks, dresses, pants, sweaters, and coats - just like dogs marking their territories. This story never sets well with women, by the way.

Here's one more tidbit about "O'Donnell's Folly" as the house became known because of O'Donnell losing his lover. During the 2008 presidential campaign, then-candidate Barack Obama spoke to supporters from one of the porches, thus inspiring the comment in his inaugural speech mentioning "from the porches of Charleston".

The Patrick O'Donnell House, 21 King St., was built in 1870.

Moving right along, after a few blocks we arrive to the peninsula's southern tip, The Battery. Touring The Battery is always a delight. The most picturesque overwhelming view of the oldest part of the city, it's perhaps the only site covered on any tour in which an array of emotions and happenings are displayed at the same time; it's like a huge theatre with numerous stages and acts being performed simultaneously. On a pleasant sunny day thousands frequent this area in awe: large chartered buses and small tour buses load and unload at the appropriate places; horse-drawn carriages touring or transporting a bride and groom can be seen; motorists slowly moving to catch a glimpse of all the surroundings; cruise and cargo ships, barges, sailboats, harbor tour boats and boats to Ft. Sumter are visibly moving in and out of the harbor; a multitude of conversations are exchanged; people of all ages leisurely walk, jog, or bike along the side streets and on High and Low Battery; fishermen yank at nibbles while spectators gather to observe; carefree lovers hold hands and exchange kisses; dolphins peek in and out of the water depending on the season; pelicans and seagulls swoop at a distance; packs of pigeons gather as humans feed them; locals are observed and admired as they enter and exit their homes and the Fort Sumter House condominium building;

and visitors enter and exit the Edmondston-Alston House Museum. White Point Gardens is the popular park that's located at The Battery. There, it's common to see wedding vows being exchanged at the gazebo, children playing on the cannons and cannonballs, folks snapping their cameras while others remain completely still to get great photographs and people relaxing on the grass and picnicking while others are relaxing on the benches. In 1993, the Rev. James Arthur Rumph, then pastor of St. James AME Church in Birmingham, AL proclaimed, "This place (The Battery) is sim-ply divine!" Yes, The Battery is a wonderful place, and you bet it's difficult at times to keep people's attention focused on their tour with all of the happenings.

The Battery got its name because of the fortifications that were placed there in the early days. Spanish, pirates and unfriendly Native Americans were constantly causes for concern and to ensure that security was tight. The area also offers a splendid view of Fort Sumter (where the Civil War began at 4:30 am on April 12, 1861 when Confederates fired from Ft. Johnson on James Island at Union-controlled Fort Sumter). Beyond Fort Sumter is the Atlantic Ocean. East Battery, South Battery and Murray Boulevard are streets that make up The Battery. The beautiful homes and mansions that line the streets are valued in the millions. Castle Pinckney is a small marsh island visible from The Battery and one of its uses was as a fort during the Civil War. Named in honor of Charles Cotesworth Pinckney, statesman and a SC signer of the US Constitution, union soldiers were imprisoned there. A common question about the fort because of the way it appears from the Battery is, "What's that bunch of green weeds in the river?"

In 2000, while conducting a tour for a senior citizen group on a chartered bus, one of the women continuously teased me; I in return continuously teased her. Knowing that the group was spending the night at a local hotel, I mentioned that The Battery has a reputation for being a lover's lane at night. I pointed my hand at the older lady and said, "This is a lover's lane at night, and tonight I better not see you down here." She looked at me and responded, "So that means you're going to be down here too!" The bus was full of laughter; I had no choice but to let her win that teasing battle.

Many visitors ask with much excitement if the body of water at The Battery is the ocean. "The ocean is nearby and this is a river," I respond. Water captivates all ages. And as for young people, once they see all that water, it's very difficult for them to remain quiet. Expressing to the adults that their excitement won't bother me eases the burden of trying to calm them down. And if it's warm and dolphins are visible, just forget the task of keeping them quiet. Some adults become as excited as the children, and some children mistake dolphins for sharks. Children are curious and adults never know what they will ask and how they will respond. I've been challenged often with various questions and remarks about the Ashley River while at The Battery: "Can we swim in that water?" "Will the dolphins eat me?" "I can jump in that water and fight those dolphins like Superman!" "Will the waves take me out to sea?" "If I jump in that water and can't swim, *my Daddy* will come and get me." "The water stinks." "What's that smell in the water?" "The water smells rotten." "How deep is that water?" and "What's that stuff in the water?"

When shifting attention away from the river, oleanders that the City has planted in the medium and next to the walkways all along Murray Blvd. and East Battery are very noticeable, especially during the summer through mid-fall when there's a gorgeous display of white and pink blooms of various hues. And yep, they are poison. Many Americans are familiar with them from coast to coast, but some have no idea that they're poisonous. In fact, even eating a small amount can cause severe illness or death to humans and animals. The sap can cause skin irritation, and inhaling smoke from burning cuttings can cause health issues as well. I've mentioned on numerous tours that some Charleston women have been known to boil oleander leaves to make a tea to poison their husbands, known as "Widow's Tea". Valerie Davis of Durham, NC said, "I have a great name for the tea for the ladies: "I Love You Honey Tea". Another woman's suggested "I Love You To Death Tea".

In the spring of 2004 while touring the Walker Family Reunion at The Battery on board a chartered bus, some of the women suddenly called out to the bus driver to stop so that they could gather oleander leaves. The men quickly

Oleander bushes are pictured in the foreground & on the right. This is the view on East Battery heading north. Many comments have been made in this area about the local saying that women used to pick these beautiful but poisonous plants for brewing a lethal hot tea to serve to their husbands.

motioned to him to keep going. Mr. Tour Guide asked the Walker women what will happen the next week if I began to receive letters and emails suddenly stating that many of the Walker men died after leaving Charleston. One of the women responded, "We'll just blame it on the She Crab Soup." Everyone laughed loudly.

Various individuals have said that it's hard to detect oleander in one's system. With that being said, some tours become shouting matches between the women and men. The women are yelling, "Stop the bus, I need to get some!" and the men are yelling, "Keep going!" Vanessa and Debbie from Detroit, MI said to me when I wouldn't stop, "You don't have to stop, keep driving your tour bus; we know where to come back to find them." I find that women are usually the more vocal ones on tours, but if there's ever a place when quiet men speak out, it's here at The Battery. Numerous divorced women have mentioned that they wish they had known about oleanders before their divorces. Mr. Tour Guide has directed this statement to many groups before stopping at The Battery, "Fellas, we have to inspect every woman's pocketbook before leaving." James Floyd from Charlotte, NC once said, "I second that motion." And can you imagine women who are part of church groups demanding to stop? "I thought you were kind Christian ladies," I've uttered numerous times in a joking manner. "Shouldn't your minds be focused on heavenly things and not evil?" Because so much emphasis is placed on what women have done or would do to men with this poisonous plant, one man thought that only males could die from them. He asked, "Will these flowers kill the women?"

Here are some other comments: In 2004, a gentleman from Inman, SC said jokingly, "I can turn the table around at my house and poison my wife because I do the cooking." When this gentleman's comments were later shared on another tour, one woman's response was, "My husband could never kill me this way; he doesn't know how to boil water." Mr. Nick from Monterey, CA said, "Mr. Al Miller, you are now giving out too much information." A race car driver said, "As far as I am concerned, you can flood it here (meaning "put the pedal to the metal") and get the hell from this area." And when Mr. Tour Guide asked Merriam Gause from Jersey City, NJ if she wanted an oleander leaf she said, "No honey, you better keep driving, my husband has the keys to the car." Her husband didn't say anything.

Now this was a first: In the summer of 2006, Brent and Ashley, a part of a family reunion group, had a very heated argument about oleanders. Ashley popped off several oleander leaves and brought them on the bus. Brent couldn't understand why she was bringing them. She kept insisting that it was just a joke and that he was too sensitive. Well, he was not buying that answer and repeatedly asked, "A joke for whom?" I was not going to get into the middle of that one, I suddenly became like my father – I just kept driving the tour bus and minded my own business. The argument soon blew over and Brent had an angry look even after the tour. During the drop off at the group's hotel, Ashley was still holding on to her oleander leaves. When I shared this couple's story later, Sharon from OK said, "In order to avoid getting into that's couple's argument and having them angry with you, you just drove the bus, huh?" Yes, Mr. Tour Guide just drove the bus. One of the worst mistakes one can make is to engage in a couple's argument. Almost always, the couple will become angry with the third party and continue to be angry, long after the lovebirds have reconciled.

Another hot topic at The Battery is a monument in White Point Gardens that's located on the corner of Murray Blvd. and East Battery. It reads "To The Confederate Defenders Of Charleston - Fort Sumter 1861-1865". Everyone notices that one of the two male figures is naked. While touring elementary and middle school children, many tend to chuckle; not because of the history, but because of the naked man that only has a leaf covering his "package". I've tried numerous times to have students to look east to see Fort Sumter, but it never works. When I hear the snickering, I know what's up. One little girl pointed at the statue from her school bus and said to her classmates, "Oh look at that man, he needs to put on some underwear." Mr. Tour Guide had to laugh himself. How intriguing it is how children express what they feel - out of the mouths of babes....

While continuing north on East Battery, we can easily see the tall brick 1808 Capt. James Misroon House at 40 East Bay St. The street changes names in this vicinity. The house was built by Misroon over a corner section of the original wall that fortified the city. The captain, an Irish businessman, owned and operated a nearby wharf. Today the former single house, that was added on in 1925, is the headquarters of Historic Charleston Foundation, one of the area's very active preservation organizations.

Often people are clustered around the state historical marker that's located in front of the Misroon House to read its text. The marker commemorates the seizure of the gunboat *Planter* by Robert Smalls, the vessel's 23-year old enslaved pilot, early morning on May 13, 1862

This SC historical marker highlighting Congressman Robert Smalls' successes was unveiled on May 12, 2012 during the City's observance of the Civil War sesquicentennial. Several of his descendants are seen on the left of the marker. Photo courtesy of the South Carolina African American Heritage Commission.

while the White crew was ashore. The boat was docked at the same wharf that Capt. Misroon had owned. Smalls bravely disguised himself as the captain and navigated the boat past Ft. Sumter. His family and some other enslaved crewmembers and their families were onboard also. They sailed out to the Atlantic Ocean and surrendered to a Navy blockade, and all were freed from enslavement. As a contract employee, Smalls piloted the *Planter* for the Navy then for the Army, and after that he became commander of the gunboat. During Reconstruction, Robert Smalls entered the political world and served as a state representative and a senator from 1868-1874, then he was elected to serve five terms in Congress. Also, Smalls had great passion for education so he created the framework that led to the establishment of South Carolina's public school system.

A bit further north on East Bay St. down from the Misroon House and on the left is the well-known Rainbow Row. Visitors regularly inquire about the location of these 18th century townhouses and/or if they'll be shown on the tour. Built as merchant houses, some as early as 1740, these adjoining buildings originally had stores downstairs and the residents lived upstairs. These buildings like many in the older part of the city can be described as "from rags to riches." In the 1930s, these houses were transformed from slums to a handsome area, and were painted in a variety of pastel colors. Rainbow Row is commonly seen on all sorts of souvenirs and visitors regularly photograph it. Also, this is the area where Dubose Heyward placed Catfish Row. The colorfulness of this section of East Bay St. is so reflective of Charleston's many connections to Barbados, along with the crape myrtle trees, cobblestone streets and single houses.

Here's the front side of the SC historical marker that's located on East Bay St. & dedicated to Congressman Robert Smalls in 2012.
A portion of the Misroon House is visible on the right of the marker.

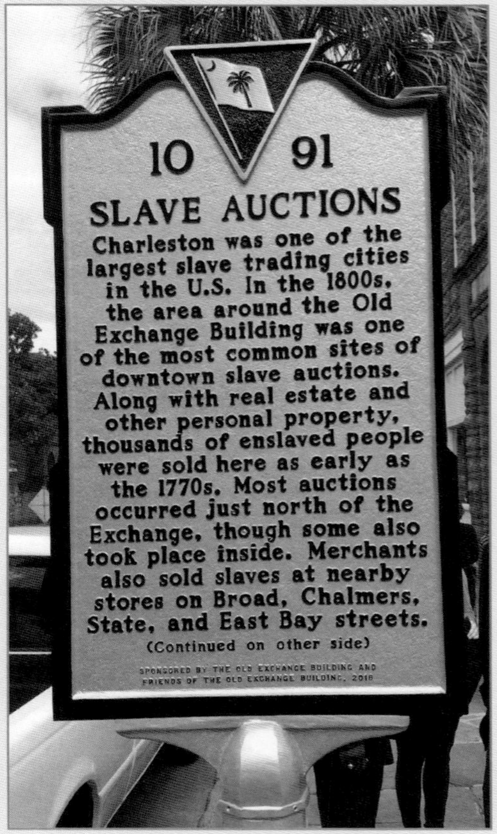

SLAVE AUCTIONS

10 91

(Continued from other side)

Enslaved Africans were usually sold at wharves along the city harbor. Some Africans were sold near the Exchange, but most people sold here were born in the U.S., making this a key site in the domestic slave trade. In 1856, the city banned auctions of slaves and other goods from the Exchange. Indoor sales grew elsewhere, and Ryan's Mart, a complex of buildings between Queen and Chalmers streets, became the main downtown auction site.

SPONSORED BY THE OLD EXCHANGE BUILDING AND FRIENDS OF THE OLD EXCHANGE BUILDING, 2016

"Slave Auctions" Historic Marker

March 10, 1853 – Slave auction occurring north of the Old Exchange Building. The Exchange is visible in the upper right hand corner.

Dedication
March 10, 2016
East Bay & Gillon streets
Charleston, South Carolina

Speakers:

Edwin Breeden, Old Exchange Building,
Rice University

Joseph McGill, Slave Dwelling Project,
Old Slave Mart Museum

On March 10, 2016, this state historical marker was unveiled on the north side of the Old Exchange & Customs House.

SLAVE AUCTIONS

10 91

Charleston was one of the largest slave trading cities in the U.S. in the 1800s. The area around the Old Exchange Building was one of the most common sites of downtown slave auctions. Along with real estate and other personal property, thousands of enslaved people were sold here as early as the 1770s. Most auctions occurred just north of the Exchange, though some also took place inside. Merchants also sold slaves at nearby stores on Broad, Chalmers, State, and East Bay streets.

(Continued on other side)

SPONSORED BY THE OLD EXCHANGE BUILDING AND FRIENDS OF THE OLD EXCHANGE BUILDING, 2016

9 | The Holy City: Churches, Churches & More Churches!

"With all these churches in Charleston, everybody should be saved!"
— *Church Group Visitor, Fall 2006*

There's a church for everyone in Charleston. Throughout my tour guide career, I've been a liaison for hundreds requesting a place of worship on Sundays or during the week. Religious preference doesn't matter, most likely there's a place of worship for everyone in the area. I've been informed countless times by visitors about houses of worship where they attended service or plan to attend while I'm giving the history of that congregation. The same has held true for attending weddings and funerals.

There's a number of church buildings in Charleston that were originally constructed for White congregations and now house Black congregations: New Tabernacle Fourth Baptist Church, 22 Elizabeth St.; Jerusalem Baptist Church, 26 Maverick St.; Centenary United Methodist Church, 60 Wentworth St.; Mt. Zion African Methodist Church, 5 Glebe St.; Tabernacle Baptist Church, 51 Gordon St. and Greater St. Luke African Methodist Episcopal Church, 78 Gordon St., for example.

Experience has taught me that when most Whites ask, "Would you recommend a good Black church?" I know that they're requesting an emotional church (singing, shouting, clapping, foot stomping, hallelujah sermons). I remember a White woman who said, "We attended that Morris Brown AME Church on Sunday, and the service was quite conservative." She enjoyed the service, but was expecting an emotion-filled one. Many have the desire to have this experience, especially internationals. When most Blacks request a place of worship, my question is: "Does it matter what denomination?" For example, if someone says that s/he prefers a Baptist church, my question would be, "Would you prefer a service that's lukewarm, hot or cold?" Some state their choice, and for some it doesn't matter as long as the "Word of God" is delivered. "We don't know about all that shouting, we better stick with a conservative service," was a response given on a tour by some relatives of the late Coretta Scott King, widow of civil rights leader Dr. Martin Luther King, Jr., who requested a church recommendation. Further, visitors of all ethnic backgrounds have asked questions about local places of worship like "Would I feel welcome?" or "What's the appropriate attire?"

Charleston is known as the "Holy City" because of its abundance of churches (over 100, representing over thirty-five different denominations located on the peninsula and in nearby annexed areas). During the early days, many immigrants came to Charleston to seek religious freedom, which was a guarantee, and some of the most beautiful architecture is found in church structures: Georgian, Greek Revival, Gothic Revival, Classic Revival, Baroque, Norman and others. Almost any denomination that comes to mind can be found in the Holy City. Each congregation has a unique history, and as a guide, Mr. Tour Guide regularly imparts tidbits about various ones in hopes that visitors will find the info both intriguing and interesting.

In some areas of the historic district, there's a church on just about every block. During the early days, sailors knew when they were approaching Charles Towne because of the tall church steeples that could be seen in the distance. The oldest denomination in Charleston is the Episcopal Church, first called the Anglican Church of England, 1681. The oldest congregation is St. Philip's Episcopal Church located at 142 Church Street and founded in 1681. The oldest church building is St. Michael's Episcopal Church at 71 Broad Street. "Is this a church tour?" one visitor shouted out many years ago. "We love the churches," a couple from the Midwest once said. Some visitors are adamant about identifying their denominations, and there are others who will remind the guide before the tour ends like the Greenwoods of New England, "You didn't show our denomination. We're Lutheran." So I gave them the history of St. Matthew's Lutheran Church, 405 King Street. They became some happy campers, fully absorbing the history of this edifice. Some tour guests have boldly expressed their opinions about their religious preferences and views; as some speak, others listen, and some keep their mouths closed to avoid a religious discussion. My mission as a guide is to give the history of the edifice and congregation and then move on. There is a familiar expression, "To avoid confusion - you don't discuss religion, politics and race."

Charleston churches create stunning settings for weddings, for locals and visitors alike; and some churches are also used regularly for concerts, recitals and programs. On any given Saturday afternoon, notably during the spring and summer, tours encounter weddings. One Saturday afternoon in the fall of 2006, my tour included glimpsing at least ten weddings. Horse drawn carriages and/or limos parked in front of various churches with attendants waiting patiently to transport the wedding parties from the church to the reception were everywhere! And better yet, catching a glimpse of a bride and groom in a horse-drawn carriage casually riding down the streets in the older part of the city results in many ooh-ahh responses from visitors. Tour Guides waving and tooting their bus horns and tourists waving at the wedding parties have always been a great gesture of admiration and well wishes. Often, wedding parties will exchange waves of acknowledgement to the tour buses. "We should find the locations of these wedding receptions and enjoy feasting on the good food and drinks. We could always claim to be distant relatives," said Marcia Adams of Ohio jokingly.

Charleston churches are also a usual scene of worshippers going to service, departing then gathering and chit-chatting afterwards. Some church folk are immaculately dressed to kill (and they know it) and others have a more simple appearance. "It's not about what you wear, but what's in your heart," has been whispered. Tourists are very observant people, and some don't miss a beat on happenings outside and inside of the bus. They notice everything about people from head to toe (the hat, dress, skirt, blouse, pants, suit, shoes, pocketbook, hairstyle and facial appearance) all while keeping up with the info being given on the bus! And if those looks had the power to kill, many would have been dead long ago. Besides, there's not an extra fee to look wherever one's heart desires on and off the tour bus. In the summer of 2006, Mr. Brian McNeal, Manager of Smith-McNeal Funeral Home, was standing in front of New Tabernacle Fourth Baptist Church, 22 Elizabeth Street, while a funeral was in session. Brian, looking cool wearing dark sunglasses, a dark suit and white shirt, greeted me as I drove slowly past the church imparting the history of it. A woman seated behind me began to whisper to her girlfriend about his good looks. I turned around and said to her with a gesture, "You're busted, and he's married." Her response was laughter with some noticeable disappointment in her voice about his being married. Finally she sighed, "Oh well…."

During some of my Black History Tours of Charleston, I have been accused by Blacks of showing too many African Methodist Episcopal Churches and United Methodist Churches. "Where are the Baptist churches?" some have questioned. Overall in America, most Blacks are Baptists, but in the Charleston area, the AME church dominates. A very popular question asked by visitors when it comes to our churches is, "Are there any integrated churches in Charleston?" My response: "Yes, of course." Many tourists agree that Charleston is like most American cities in that the integrated churches are usually either non-denominational, Catholic or Kingdom Halls of Jehovah's Witnesses, for example. Most churches have few members of the opposite race. One German lady who was a Jehovah's Witness couldn't understand "why do churches have to be separated? Why can't we all attend the same church and be unified as one?" Then "Amen!" and "Hallelujah!" rang out to this most revealing remark - "Churches are the most segregated places in America on Sundays." Occasionally, tourists will express concern and ask if they would be welcomed by certain churches because of their race.

In the Charleston area, it was not unusual for Blacks and Whites to worship under the same roofs in White churches prior to Emancipation. Enslaved Blacks were forced to worship in the balconies and galleries of White churches. Some free Blacks purchased their own pews and worshipped on the bottom level with Whites. In some of the more rural churches, many congregants worshipped on the same pews. In addition, some enslaved Blacks secretly practiced their native religions. Many enslaved people were converted to Protestantism because their owners required it. Further, some planters allowed their enslaved Africans to conduct their own services.

Black congregations such as Memorial Baptist Church, 153 Alexander Street; Morris Street Baptist Church, 25 Morris Street; Centenary United Methodist Church, 60 Wentworth Street and Calvary Baptist Church, 620 Rutledge Avenue originated in White churches and established their own churches after the Civil War

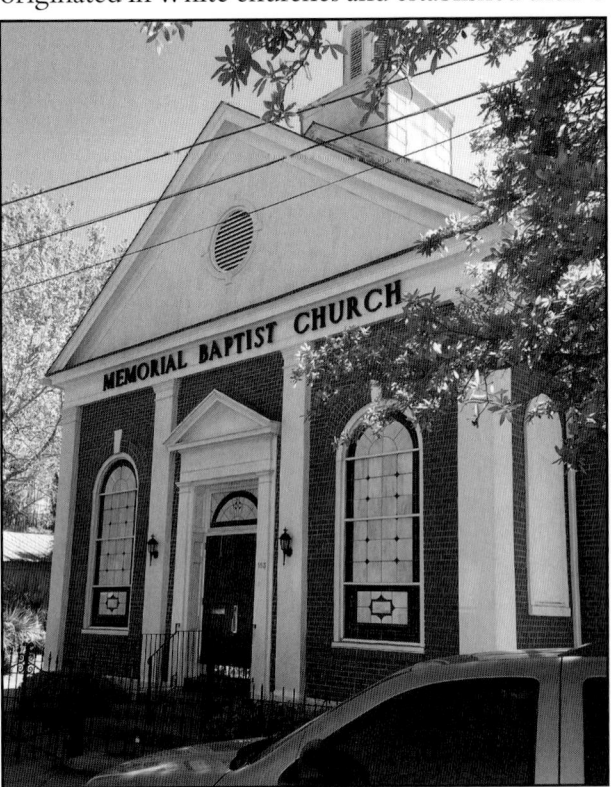

Here's info on some of the other churches on the Charleston peninsula:

Bethel United Methodist Church at Pitt and Calhoun Streets, a White congregation, and *Old Bethel United Methodist Church*, diagonally across from it at 222 Calhoun Street, a Black congregation, often summon the remark "interesting" when visitors hear about their connected histories. During slavery, Old Bethel stood on the spot of the present day Bethel where Blacks and Whites worshipped together. After the Civil War, Bethel's congregation built a new church and gave the old church to its Black members who then rolled it across the street on palmetto logs to its present location. The older church was built in 1797, making it the third oldest church building in the city.

Memorial Baptist Church was built c. 1886 and renovated in the 1970s. Black Baptists left First Baptist Church on Church St. after the Civil War and formed a new congregation in 1886.

The *Cathedral of St. John the Baptist*, 122 Broad Street, was built in 1890 from Connecticut brownstone. This stunning and picturesque Roman Catholic cathedral has been described as being patterned after German Gothic churches of the 14th century. The original church was built on this location in 1854 and was destroyed by the Great Fire of 1861. This breathtaking edifice is one that's frequently used for weddings throughout the year.

Central Baptist Church, 26 Radcliffe Street, was built in 1891, one year after the Cathedral, and was designed by John P. Hutchinson, a Black architect. Hutchinson was biracial, his father Isaac Jenkins Mikell was a wealthy Edisto Island planter. The interior of this wooden structure contains murals painted in 1912 by artist Amohamed Milai of Calcutta, India. For numerous years, just like Mt. Zion AME Church, Central's worship was conservative; very little emotion was expressed from the congregation prior to the 1980s. I heard a Mrs. Taylor say, "When I was a child, Central Church was not cold, it was ice cold." Mrs. Taylor's remark led to this explosive comment by someone else on the bus: "Everybody doesn't worship the same. There's a church for everyone."

First Scots Presbyterian Church, 53 Meeting Street, was organized in 1731, and the present edifice was built in 1814. It's the fifth oldest house of worship in Charleston. The seal of the Church of Scotland is in the window over the main entrance. "And it's one of the churches in Charleston that does not have bells, the bells were loaned to the Confederate army during the Civil War and were never replaced," added Sophia, a Canadian who heard this information on another tour.

Grace Episcopal Church, 100 Wentworth Street, is another breathtaking structure that's received with an overwhelming response from visitors. Built in 1847 in the Gothic Revival style, the goal of the founders was to build a church in the center of the city, and Wentworth Street was in the center at the time. Many consider Grace to be a "must photograph".

Kahal Kadosh Beth Elohim, 90 Hasell Street, is the birthplace of Reform Judaism in the US and the oldest surviving Reform synagogue in the world. Built in 1840, it's the second oldest synagogue building in the United States and the oldest in continuous use (Touro Synagogue in Newport, RI built in 1759 is the oldest Jewish house of worship in the US, but not in continuous use.) This structure is one of the finest examples of Greek Revival Style architecture in the city, and it replaced the original building that was built on this site in 1749. The original synagogue burned in the Great Fire of 1838. Jews arrived in Charles Towne shortly after it was settled. The Coming Street Jewish Cemetery is the oldest Jewish burial ground in the South.

Morris Brown African Methodist Episcopal Church, 13 Morris Street, was organized in 1867, and named for Charlestonian the Rev. Morris Brown, the founder of the African Methodist Episcopal Church in SC and the second Bishop of the AME Church. Morris Brown College in Atlanta, GA is also named for him. When I came to Charleston in 1974, I often listened to their Sunday worship service on WPAL Radio. Later during my college days I was told that this large congregation's nickname was "The Flower Garden" because many of the ladies were in competition with each other with their elegant attire. In 2001, a Black woman who left Charleston over 60 years before and migrated to NY said, "I think that's the church where the women wore those big hats when I was a child."

Morris Brown Church was used regularly for meetings and programs during the Civil Rights Movement.

Morris Street Baptist Church, 25 Morris Street, was organized in 1865 from a two-room building on Morris Street and became the "Mother Church Among Negro Baptists in Charleston". The building was also used for meetings and programs during the Civil Rights Movement. Further, this is the home church of Harvey B. Gantt, architect and first Black mayor of Charlotte, NC (1983-1987). Born in Charleston in 1943, Gantt was also the first Black student to attend Clemson University in 1963, and his wife Lucinda Brawley was the second. Gantt's relatives are active members of Morris Street Baptist. "You learn something new all the time, don't you? We're from Charlotte and didn't know that Harvey Gantt's from Charleston." Some visitors have remarked with just one word - "Wild!". And speaking of Charlotte, the Harvey B. Gantt Center for African-American Arts + Culture (formerly the Afro-American Cultural Center) has celebrated the contributions of Africans and African Americans to the US for over four decades. It serves as a community epicenter for music, dance, theater, visual art, film, arts education programs, literature and outreach.

Mt. Zion African Methodist Episcopal Church, 5 Glebe Street, was built 1847 in the Baroque style as the Glebe Street Presbyterian Church; and it later became Zion Presbyterian Church. Zion merged with another congregation, and the building was purchased in 1882 by a group of elite Blacks who left Emanuel AME on Calhoun Street. According to numerous Black Charlestonians, this elite group told the others as they left Emanuel to organize Mt. Zion, "If a comb cannot go straight through your hair, you are not free to worship with us. And for those tied-head mammies, let's leave them behind." This congregation, having been very conservative in its worship until the 1970's, did not clap their hands, pat their feet, nor said "Amen". If these emotions were heard and seen, the members would look at each other and whisper, "Must be a visitor." This tidbit of history on Mt. Zion has been passed down through the years and is always a conversation piece on the tour bus. The stiffness of the congregation in the past does not set well with most visitors. Therefore, some quickly have their say like Elsie Ford from Silver Spring, MD who quipped: "So they were too cute and proper to get emotional?" Janice Lewis from a Baptist church group from Tyler, TX protested, "I couldn't have gone to this Church!" On numerous tours many have agreed on churches in their cities that were just like Mt. Zion. "What would have happened if the Spirit would have really hit them?" Jeffrey Conley of Atlanta, GA posed. "How could they get the Spirit? They didn't have any!" replied Terry Battle from Los Angeles, CA. Today, the church congregation has a wonderful choir and they clap their hands, pat their feet and say "Amen." Some visitors think this edifice is a part of the College of Charleston since most buildings on Glebe Street are owned by the College. Mt. Zion is one of just a few of the Black congregations remaining in Charleston where traditional music is played: hymns, anthems and spirituals. Also, you can put on your shouting shoes while being entertained by the Mt. Zion Spiritual Singers at their concert entitled "Old Camp Meeting" that's presented annually during Charleston's Spoleto Festival. This electrifying foot-stomping concert receives rave reviews.

Old Church of the Redeemer at 32 N. Market Street in the City Market was built in 1916 by the Charleston Port Society so that seamen would have a place to worship. Once known as the Seamen's Church, it's presently two eateries. When entering this structure one might say, "Well I'll be darned, let's eat and not worship." The exterior still resembles a church, complete with stained glass.

St. John's Lutheran Church, 10 Archdale Street, is Charleston's oldest Lutheran congregation (1742). During the American Revolution, the pastor of the church, Rev. John Nicholas Martin, refused to pray for the King of England; so he was expelled from the city and his property was confiscated by the British. The present edifice was built in 1816. Dr. John Bachman, a native of Rhinebeck, NY, a theological leader and scientist, served as pastor of the church for 59 years (1815-1874). He also served as the first Professor of Natural History at the College of Charleston (1848-1853). He founded the South Carolina Lutheran Synod in Pomaria, SC in 1830, the Lutheran Theological Southern Seminary (today in Columbia, SC) and Newberry College, Newberry, SC in 1856. Dr. Bachman also trained the first Black ministers in Lutheranism such as Daniel Alexander Payne (born in Charleston, SC), who later became the sixth Bishop of the AME Church and President of Wilberforce University in Ohio; Boston Jenkins Drayton, a member and lay minister of the Black congregation of St. John Lutheran who later was sent to Liberia, West Africa by the Church as a missionary; and Jehu Jones, Jr., a member of the church who became the first Black ordained Lutheran minister in North America (1832). His father Jehu Jones, Sr. owned and operated an exclusive hotel in Charleston on Broad St. that only catered to influential Whites, as discussed in Chapter 8.

St. Mark's Episcopal Church, 14 Thomas Street, was founded in 1865 by some members of the Brown Fellowship Society, the elite benevolent organization of light-skinned or brown Black men. The church was erected in 1875 in the Greek Revival style at a cost of $15,000. Like Centenary United Methodist Church, many of the original members were free Blacks, descendants of free Blacks and Black slave masters before Emancipation. They were among the wealthiest and more prominent Blacks in the city. Some of the prominent families in St. Mark's were the Walls, Maxwells, Mushingtons, Kinlochs, Leslies, DaCostas, Montgomerys, Dereefs, McKinlays, Bennetts, O'Hears, Greggs, Houstons, and Bosemans. The congregation was mainly multi-racial individuals who were just as color conscious as they were class conscious. Tradition says that St. Mark's is where the brown bag and comb tests were performed - one would place a brown paper bag next to his/her face. If the person was darker than the bag, he/she was not free to worship there. The comb had to slide easily through one's hair in order to pass that test.

St. Mary's Roman Catholic Church, 95 Hasell Street, is the Mother Church of Catholicism for the Carolinas and Georgia. Established in 1789, most of its original members were French immigrants, and that explains why many of the tombstones in the churchyard are written in French. Also, the parish registers were kept in French until 1822. The first church was burned in the Great Fire of 1838, and the present edifice was completed in 1839.

The *Unitarian Church*, 4 Archdale Street and next to St. John's Lutheran, is the second oldest church edifice in the city and is the oldest Unitarian Church in the South. It was originally built to house the overflow of the Circular Congregational Church on Meeting St. Now, here's a tidbit for you Harvard alumni - Dr. Samuel Gilman, a New Englander and Harvard grad, served as pastor from 1819 to 1858. He wrote his alma mater's anthem, "Fair Harvard"! Mrs. Gilman published and edited *The Rosebud,* the first children's newspaper in the US. They're both buried in the churchyard. In 2013, the church erected a monument to honor the enslaved artisans who built the church. One visitor, a college professor, commented in early 2017, "Too bad it doesn't say: 'In memory of those skilled African artisans, while held in bondage, made these bricks, laid them artfully, and helped build our church c 1774 -1787'."

Above In Sept. 2013, this 3x4 foot monument was dedicated in the Unitarian Church cemetery honoring the enslaved craftsmen who made the bricks and built the church. The inscription on the base reads, "In memory of those enslaved workers who made these bricks and helped build our church c 1774-1787." Original colonial-era bricks from the church were reused to create the memorial.

The site of *Zion Presbyterian Church*, built in 1859, was 123 Calhoun St. It was located where the Courtyard Marriot Hotel is presently. Zion was the largest brick church in Charleston seating 2,500. It was largely devoted to mission work, and had a predominantly Black congregation. Zion Presbyterian merged with Olivet Presbyterian Church in 1959, forming Zion-Olivet Presbyterian, formerly located at 134 Cannon Street. The Calhoun Street structure was demolished in 1961. The City of Charleston placed one of its annual historic site designation plaques at the church's site during the 1990 Moja Arts Festival. It's located at the front of the property, very close to the street.

Black churches have become a hot topic relating to discrimination. Linda, a light-skinned Black woman from Cleveland, Ohio who apparently inherited her complexion from her mother, uttered, "Let's talk about these churches: When my parents were married, my father who was dark complexioned could not become a member of my mother's church because he was too dark." She went on to say that through the years as the older members died and attitudes changed, her father finally joined. So this question was directed to Linda, "Your parents' marriage lasted, didn't it?" Linda responded, "Of course, my mother never left my father; she knew what she was getting when she married him, she knew he was dark and he was who she wanted and who she loved." Mae of Bradenton, FL with her dark-skinned husband seated next to her commented, "Yes of course your mother knew what she was getting. Look at my husband, he's dark. The darker the berry honey, the sweeter the juice."

Comments on skin complexion have made ears sizzle on the tour bus, more on this hot topic in Book Three.

TOURISTS CAN SAY THE DARNDEST THINGS!

A female tourist said that her brother told her this joke before passing away: "There were three men who died and went to Heaven. They struck up a conversation, curious to know what each one had died from while on Earth. The first man said, "I died from diabetes." The second man said, "I died from a massive heart attack." The third man said, "I died from seen us." The other men asked, "Seen us, what in the world is that?" He responded, "I was out with another man's wife and he seen us."

It's very common to see gas lights burning at the entrances to many of the homes in the historic district depicting the flavor of times past. As gas prices rose during the spring and summer of 2008, some of the residences discontinued this practice while others continued. As the tour bus cruised through the lower peninsula area one day, a woman from Illinois said, "I don't believe these people are constantly burning gas as expensive as it is." Another woman followed up and said, "I know that's right, I need to get some of this gas to put in my car!"

Also in 2008, a woman shared this about her grandmother in Louisiana: "She was very fair (light-skinned) and didn't like any Blacks who were dark-skinned. She would sit on her porch, cross her legs, fold her arms and when dark-skinned Black people would walk by, grandmother would whisper - 'Look, should we kill them now or should we let them go?'"

10 | The Eastside

As we inch our way back to the Visitor Center via East Bay St., we'll revisit some of the French Quarter, Ansonborough and Mazyck-Wraggborough, then we'll explore a bit of the area that was once known as the Village of Hampstead.

Meanwhile, at the northwest corner of East Bay and George Sts. in Ansonborough is a late 19th century double house that was the home of the John F. and Mary S. Grimké family. Two of their fourteen children were well-known

The Blake- Grimké House at 321 East Bay St. was the childhood home of abolitionists/women's rights activists Sarah & Angelina Grimké. Sue Monk Kidd, author of "The Secret Life of Bees" and "Invention of Wings" was present during the 2015 historical marker dedication. "Invention of Wings" centers around the Grimké sisters.

abolitionists and women's rights advocates, Sarah Moore Grimké and Angelina Grimké Weld. Another well-known family member was Archibald Grimké, Sarah and Angelina's nephew. His father was their brother Henry, and his mother was Nancy Weston, who was enslaved by Henry. Archibald lived and worked successfully away from Charleston as a lawyer, author, editor and politician. And like his aunts, he spoke out against and wrote about issues that he was passionate about - primarily promoting African American rights and denouncing racism. In addition, Archibald's brother Francis, also Nancy and Henry's son, was a Presbyterian minister, lecturer and a Howard University (Washington, DC) trustee. A state historical marker was unveiled on the George St. side of this c.1789 structure in May 2015.

Mazyck-Wraggborough is a part of Charleston's Eastside and is currently a consolidated neighborhood, formerly two suburbs named after Alexander Mazyck and Joseph Wragg, original land owners. Mazyckborough was surveyed and laid out in 1786. Wraggborough came into existence when Wragg's children and grandchildren had the land that they inherited surveyed and laid out in 1801. They then named the streets after Joseph's children: Ann, Charlotte, Elizabeth, Henrietta, John, Judith and Mary. This bit of information tends to surprise many locals who have resided and traveled on these streets all of their lives, and had no clue to the origin of the names. This section was incorporated into the City of Charleston after 1850; prior to that, it was a part of the larger area known as the Neck. Today, the Charleston Neck is the area at the peninsula's extreme northern end and extending to the City of North Charleston.

While heading north on Elizabeth St. from Calhoun St., we'll approach a fascinating church on the right: New Tabernacle Fourth Baptist Church, # 22. It was constructed in 1859 in the Gothic Revival style and designed in the shape of a Greek cross. Further, it has thirty-seven feet high windows, great acoustics and its earthquake bolts are shaped like fan blades. The present congregation was established by the Rev. Daniel J. Jenkins in 1875, and it purchased this building in 1950 from St. Luke Episcopal Church. St. Luke merged with St. Paul in 1949, and is presently the Cathedral of St. Luke and St. Paul Episcopal Church, located in Radcliffeborough. Fourth Baptist's congregation moved from a structure on the city's west side when the Medical College of South Carolina (now the Medical University of South Carolina) began expanding. Know also that the Rev. Jenkins founded the Jenkins Orphanage in 1891, Charleston's first orphanage for African American children.

Fourth Baptist's pastor is the Rev. Francis Covington and *"he can preach!"* many would agree. He's an emotional minister and so is the congregation. His wife, Mrs. Judy Drumming Covington was quoted once in Edna's Beauty Shop on Cannon Street as saying, "Tell those folks (meaning the tourists) that I'm one of those minister's wives who don't wear those big hats to church." You see, some women's hats are so huge, if you sit behind them, you can't see the preacher - or anyone else. And speaking of wearing hats to church, this is still a tradition in the Black community, especially among the elders. Many elders will tell you quickly that they "don't feel right" going to church without a hat. I remember attending a wake service for a fraternity brother's mother. She was wearing her hat in the casket! Her son stated at the wake service, "Mama never went to church without a hat on her head and *insisted* wearing one after death. She always said that her children *better* have a hat on her head, and this is what you see."

The Aiken-Rhett House, 48 Elizabeth St., is a museum house that's owned by the Historic Charleston Foundation. It's the organization that's housed in the Misroon House that I discussed in Chapter Eight. During my earlier tenure as a guide, I was employed briefly by American Sightseeing Tours, and visits to the Aiken-Rhett House and the Joseph Manigault House on Meeting St. were a part of the tour. It was imperative to know the history of these houses in order to save time on busy days rather than have to depend on the house guides to conduct the tour.

The house was built in 1820 and purchased in 1827 by William Aiken, Sr. who was the president and founder of the South Carolina Canal and Rail Road Company. Aiken, an Irish immigrant, used the house as rental property. After his death, this 23-room mansion was inherited by his only son, William Aiken, Jr. William Jr. was a SC governor, US Congressman, rice planter, and he was also one of the largest slaveholders in SC. As a result of his various business dealings, he was one of the state's wealthiest citizens. He owned more than 700 enslaved African Americans just on his Jehossee rice plantation, located on the south Edisto River southwest of Charleston. William Jr. and his wife Harriet Lowndes Aiken moved into the house in 1833. When they married, they went on a five-year honeymoon and shopping spree to Europe and purchased a great deal of furniture. Their daughter Henrietta Aiken Rhett and her descendants inherited the house. Frances Dill Rhett gave it to the Charleston Museum in 1975, which owned it until 1995.

The Aiken-Rhett House was built c. 1820 and is a museum today.

These are some historical tidbits that docents have shared with visitors that I've taken to tour the house:

- There was a painting of Mrs. Aiken in the drawing room that she hated. The artist drew her much larger than she really was. Very conscious of her weight, some days Mrs. Aiken would only eat one meal or very little, all hoping to maintain her ninety pounds.
- Mrs. Aiken's bedroom was closed for seventy-nine years after her death. When the room was reopened in the early 1970s, the dust in it was eighteen inches thick! Cary Clover from WV snickered, "I hope her body wasn't left in the room after seventy-nine years!" Another visitor said, "That sounds like my house." A gentleman replied while glancing at his teenage daughter, "No, no, no! That sounds like my daughter's room." On another tour, a visitor said to her husband who took a quick glimpse at her, "Honey, *don't you say a word.*"
- The Aikens' only daughter married William Rhett. The Rhetts had five children - four sons and one daughter. It was okay for that daughter to marry; however, whenever the sons mentioned marriage, Mrs. Rhett would become ill and remain ill for two to three weeks. Two of her sons caught on to her games and married without her consent. They were banned from the house for five years.
- The oldest son, I'on Rhett, dated Frances Dill of James Island for twenty-five years. Some said that he was waiting for his mother to die. She died at age eighty-three. The couple married after her death, both being nearly sixty years old and too old to have children. A gentleman from PA commented in 2004 followed by a large chuckle, "I'on Rhett was not a Strom Thurmond." He was referring to the SC politician who fathered four children in his senior years from 1971 – 1976. He died at age 100 in 2003.
- Many locals called Frances Dill Rhett, the last descendant to live in the house, "the old lady". She would invite her friends over to play cards. On rainy nights, the house leaked. Mrs. Rhett ignored the leaks and continued to play cards.
- When Mrs. Rhett passed away, the two drawing rooms were closed for fifty-three years, and only opened once for a wedding.
- Guides are always observant of their surroundings. In 1987, a male guide was conducting the tour for my group and others. It was a warm day, and suddenly the guide noticed that a young woman was about to pass out from the heat. We were told that she was on her honeymoon. The guide said later, "She was probably not only exhausted from the heat, but from the honey as well, if you know what I mean."

The two outbuildings or dependencies located at the rear of the house are visible as we ride north on Elizabeth St. then turn east onto Mary St. The building away from the street consisted of the slave quarters upstairs and the kitchen and laundry rooms downstairs. The building closest to the street consisted of more slave quarters upstairs with the stable and carriage house below. The slits at the bottom of the building were for ventilation. The family allowed their cows and chickens to roam freely in the courtyard during the day, then they were housed in the stable at night.

Two outbuildings or dependencies are located at the rear of the main house. Enslaved African Americans were quartered upstairs over the kitchen/laundry and stable/carriage house. Note the vertical ventilation slit near the bottom of the building that's at the right of the wall.

The courtyard was used to film a scene in the mini-series *North and South* in the 1980s. In 2007, the house was repainted its original color. A local Black gentleman on the bus who was a member of a family reunion group said that he was one of the painters. "They ran out of paint before reaching the slave quarters," he mentioned.

Let's head further into the Eastside. The America St. public housing apartments were built in the 1940s. "None of the public housing communities we've seen in Charleston has bad appearances," noted the Jakeses from OH. One popular consensus is that not only are the various public housing communities nice looking, Charleston's streets are clean. Often there have been complaints about the city's uneven and bumpy streets through the years, however - "With all the money this city makes from tourism, some of the streets need to be repaired," is one of the comments that comes to mind.

The Village of Hampstead was part of a large land parcel owned and named by Henry Laurens around 1769. He subdivided it into one-hundred forty lots and laid out the area reflecting seventeenth- and eighteenth-century English suburbs. Laurens, incidentally, was a successful merchant and a partner in one of the largest "slave trading houses" in North America. He enslaved about three hundred people at Mepkin, his rice plantation on the Cooper River; that plantation is now a monastery. Laurens was also president of the Continental Congress from 1777-1778. There's a Laurens St. in Ansonborough as well as a SC city and county named after him.

Hampstead drew planters, merchants, artisans, laborers and a number of free Black families who purchased lots there in the eighteenth and nineteenth centuries. Among the planters who bought property were quite a few from Georgetown, SC, about sixty miles from Charleston. Among the artisans and laborers were a carpenter, butcher, lumber smith and wig maker. Among the free Blacks were businessmen like Jehu Jones, Richard Dereef, Richard Holloway and Thomas Bonneau.

We can get a distinct reminder of the Caribbean in Hampstead too. As we cruise down America St., there are a number of colorful Charleston single houses. Single houses are "one room wide with a porch on the side" as the saying goes. This architectural style is prevalent throughout Charleston, in older and newer neighborhoods. Most single houses have porches, and the porches (also called piazzas or verandas) usually face to the south or west in order to capture the best river breezes. There are several theories as to where Charlestonians adopted this building style from, but the more common belief is that the single house was transplanted here from Barbados, where numerous other local traditions originated. The colorfulness of the homes and other structures definitely gives a West Indian flair as well.

At the corner of America and Reid Sts., there's a stop sign. In the 1990s while touring a family reunion group on their bus, I didn't feel the bus come to a stop. It was drifting at a very slow pace - the driver had dozed off and just went on through the stop sign! No one on the bus noticed because everybody was taken aback by the house that I'm about to discuss. Mr. Tour Guide whispered into the driver's ear, "*James, you need to wake up!*"

On this corner, there's a quaint little house that's a replica of a Charleston single house, but a mini version. It was built as a public art exhibit during the 1991 Spoleto Festival USA. "Is that a house? Do people really live in that house?" are the most common questions that visitors ask. Now, I never said that people lived in this house, I said that it was an art exhibit. People become so fascinated with it that they make lots of commotion and snap lots of photos. One New Yorker said, "If this house was in NY, the homeless would be living in it."

Occasionally, visitors mention witnessing some drug activity in Hampstead, or at least what *appears* to them as being a drug deal in the process. I remember when one lady began to ask a host of questions about drugs in the neighborhood. As she began to ask the fifth question, Mr. Tour Guide said to her, "Ma'am, would you like for me to stop the bus and get you a nickel bag or what?" She responded, "No, I'm just asking questions." Mr. Tour Guide said, "And I'm just asking *you* a question." New Yorker Lloyd later said, "What the heck, she probably wanted a quarter bag." When I repeated this story on another tour, Mark responded, "I didn't know you could still get a nickel bag." Upon arriving at the corner of America and Columbus Sts., a statue of the late Philip Simmons is visible in Hampstead Square. The statue was located at a nearby house and was relocated

Tourists Can Say the Darndest Things!

when the house was sold. It's been said that the Square was selected for its new home because Mr. Simmons often sat there to watch children play. The City of Charleston rededicated the statue in March 2015. See a photo of the Simmons statue at the end of this chapter.

Our Lady of Mercy Roman Catholic Church, founded in 1928, is at 77 America St. Some visitors remark that they see few Catholic churches in Charleston, well here's one of the five that's in the city. Hampstead Mall is across from the church and was the focal point of the Village of Hampstead. I remember during one trek through the Eastside, Ms. Birch from Albany, NY said with a smile and enthusiasm, "Oh yes! We're in the hood now. But, this is all good and beautiful; you need to see the bad and the good to understand the entire picture. Charleston is more than about just pretty houses, and I see nice houses and history in this neighborhood as well. The other tour we took certainly did *not* bring us over here. You have good and bad people everywhere." And by the way, some international visitors as well as some American Whites often ask what "the hood" means.

"The House of the Future" was designed in 1991 by NY artist David Hammons for a city-wide Spoleto Festival USA exhibit called *Places with a Past*. Nineteen artists were involved. The neighborhood chose to keep this installation after the exhibit ended.

When we turn onto Blake St. from America St., #30 ½ is our focus, the late Philip Simmons' home and workshop. When Mr. Simmons was alive, he would greet everyone with open arms who came to see his home and workshop. He was very patient even when scheduled groups were late. Mr. Simmons was always a delight to meet, and everybody just loved him, young and old. He said to a group in 2005, "I don't do this work anymore; I just smile before the camera." He's been described as being a jewel and as being just like old mahogany - they don't make people like him anymore. In 2004, I had the privilege of bringing the Walker family reunion to meet Mr. Simmons. He looked at me and said with a smile, "You're not a Walker!" He had a great sense of humor, was full of knowledge and wisdom, and was very down to earth. He was often asked if he were rich. Mr. Simmons' response was, "Yes, I'm rich with all the knowledge and wisdom God has given me." Charleston's treasured blacksmith was placed in an assisted living facility on James Island in 2008, and he passed away in June 2009 at age 97. Presently, the 840 square foot c. 1890 house that Mr. Simmons bought in 1959 is a museum operated by the foundation bearing his name.

Directly in front of the Philip Simmons house museum is the back of the Palmer Campus of Trident Technical College which is headquartered in North Charleston. In August 2008, the Palmer Campus opened up the Culinary Institute of Charleston that offers training in the hospitality industry. The former Charles A. Brown High School was located where the Blake St. section of Trident Tech's campus is located presently. C. A. Brown High was briefly named Eastside High School when it opened in September 1962. The school was one of many local examples of maintaining separate but equal educational facilities in order to avoid integration. When White school board chairman Charles A. Brown died, the high school was renamed after him shortly after the 1962-1963 school year started as a memorial to him and to his many dedicated years to public education. C. A. Brown High provided an educational foundation for Black students on this side of the city until it was closed in 1982. The school then merged with Burke High, its former rival, located on the city's west side.

When we turn right onto Drake Street, a very large brick building is on the left called the Old Cigar Factory. It extends all the way down the block to Columbus St. This historic building is bordered by Drake St. to the west, Columbus St. to the south, Blake St. to the north and East Bay St. to the east.

Originally operating as a cotton mill from November 1882-May 1900, the American Tobacco Company leased the building in 1903, then bought it in 1912. By the 1940s, profits were large and so was its workforce. Employees were segregated by race and gender, and females were in the majority. In the fall of 1945, workers at three American Tobacco Company plants, and with strong union support, decided to strike. Charleston workers demanded back pay that was withheld during World War II, higher wages, medical benefits, mandatory employee union membership and non-discrimination clauses to end hiring, firing and employee treatment biases. The other two factories were located in Philadelphia, PA and Trenton, NJ. In Charleston, Black and White men and women showed solidarity and pushed for change; however, most White men eventually inched away from protesting because those who had skilled positions knew that gender and racial discrimination were benefits to them and made their jobs secure.

Meanwhile, as Charleston striking workers continued to gather and retain support for their cause among each other and the community, an African American female employee changed the spiritual *I Will Overcome Someday* to *We Will Overcome* and revised some of the lyrics. It became the anthem for the strike. The song's lyrics and title were revised again at the Highlander Folk School in TN in the late 1940s. *We Shall Overcome* became a leading protest mantra, especially during the height of the Civil Rights Movement in the 1950s-1960s. The Cigar Factory strike lasted until March 1946 when management conceded to some of the workers' demands. In addition, the workers felt empowered realizing that persistence and solidarity worked to further their cause and that their organized efforts resulted in their voices being heard. The factory closed in 1973 as a result of the laws on tobacco companies becoming more strict and a decrease in tobacco use. The building was then used for awhile as warehouse and office spaces. The culinary school, Johnson and Wales University, became a large tenant in the 1980s until the school moved its campus to Charlotte, NC in 2006. A developer bought the building in 2007 for twenty million dollars and envisioned reworking the structure to house condos above retail and office spaces. That project failed, and a group of about ten investors purchased it in 2014 for $24.18 million. Approximately fifty-five million dollars later, the block-long structure opened in the fall of 2015 as a mixed-use endeavor with businesses and an events venue.

This is side 2 of a state historical marker that was erected in 2013 at the former cigar factory. It documents the building's history, including the 1945-1946 workers' strike.

Now, let's briefly travel south on East Bay St. then ride through Mazyck-Wraggborough via Chapel St., and I'll point out a couple of my favorite homes before we arrive back at the Visitor Center. The Elias Vanderhorst (pronounced Vandross) mansion, #28, was built about 1832. Incidentally, this family owned much of what's now Kiawah Island, a popular resort island located next to Johns Island, about 26 miles from Charleston. The Vanderhorst plantation was a major rice-growing operation. Notice the double stairway with stone steps leading to the piazza with curved iron side railings. This stairway style is often described as "elbow" or "embracing arms". Many visitors, both males and females, describe this stairway as "elegant".

Dr. H. Vanderhorst Toomer was the appointed physician for the Charleston Neck in the 1850s. He lived at #34 Chapel and died in 1858 while tending to patients of Charleston's great yellow fever epidemic of that year. The house was built around 1840 on a high basement and has a curving piazza that makes the house unique. The front steps used to have greenery growing along the railings. If this house were located in a country setting, those afraid of snakes would have been skeptical of walking up the steps during the summer because of "being afraid of being kissed by snakes," as one tourist described. Because of all of the ranting and

The Cigar Factory at 701 East Bay St. opened in 2015 as a mixed-use building after major renovations by private investors.

raving over this sophisticated piece of real estate, Mr. Tour Guide doesn't have to ask if anyone wants to take a picture, it's usually a given. Furthermore, you won't find many Charleston houses with underground basements because of the city's low altitude. This is why the term "Low Country" (also spelled low country,

The Elias Vanderhorst House at 28 Chapel St. was built c. 1832.

Lowcountry and lowcountry) is used prevalently in this part of the state. "Do you bury the dead above ground like in New Orleans?" is a very popular question. Nope, most burials are under the ground in Charleston.

The Dr. Anthony Vanderhorst Toomer House at 34 Chapel St. was built c. 1840 by either Dr. A.V. Toomer or his son Dr. H.V. Toomer.

A v-shaped park is just down the street from these two houses that create a split in Chapel St. at the corner of Elizabeth St. It was the site of a chapel that was built there in 1858 and used as interim worship sites by two congregations. The chapel was demolished in 1884. Chapel St. got its name though because of a nearby plot of land that was allocated for a chapel when Wraggborough was laid out in 1801, but that chapel was never built. Note that the street's name changes to John St. as soon as we cross through the Elizabeth St. intersection.

We're almost back to the Visitor Center, and as we approach the intersection of John and Meeting Sts., there's an eye-catching site coming up on the right. A replica of the Confederate submarine *H.L. Hunley* sets in front of The Charleston Museum. The sub attacked the *USS Housatonic* near Sullivan's Island, east of Charleston, in February 1864 and sank it. However, the *Hunley* was swept up in the explosion's wake and sank also. This episode was the first time that a submarine had ever destroyed an enemy ship. The *Hunley* was discovered in the Atlantic Ocean in 1995 and was resurfaced in 2000. Presently, it's kept at a conservatory in North Charleston on the former naval base.

The *H.L. Hunley* replica & The Charleston Museum are located across Meeting St. from the Charleston Visitor Reception and Transportation Center. The *Hunley* was the first submarine to sink an enemy ship. The Charleston Museum, founded in 1773, is known as "America's First Museum".

In Memory Of The Late Mr. Philip Simmons - A Low Country Legacy

PHILIP SIMMONS (1912 – 2009)

PHILIP SIMMONS WAS THE MOST CELEBRATED OF CHARLESTON IRONWORKERS OF THE 20TH CENTURY. BORN ON DANIEL ISLAND, HE MOVED TO THIS AREA AND ENROLLED AT BUIST ELEMENTARY SCHOOL AT THE AGE OF EIGHT. HE RECEIVED HIS MOST INFLUENTIAL EDUCATION FROM A LOCAL BLACKSMITH WHO RAN A BUSY SHOP AT THE FOOT OF CALHOUN STREET. IT WAS THERE THAT SIMMONS ACQUIRED THE VALUES AND REFINED THE TALENTS THAT WOULD SUSTAIN HIM THROUGH HIS LONG METALWORKING CAREER, MOVING INTO THE SPECIALIZED FIELD OF ORNAMENTAL IRON IN 1938, SIMMONS EVENTUALLY FASHIONED MORE THAN 500 DECORATIVE WROUGHT-IRON PIECES INCLUDING GATES, FENCES, BALCONIES AND WINDOW GRILLS, FROM RIVER TO RIVER AND END TO END, THE CITY OF CHARLESTON IS TRULY DECORATED BY HIS HAND.

AMONG HIS MANY HONORS, SIMMONS RECEIVED THE NATIONAL HERITAGE FELLOWSHIP FROM THE NATIONAL ENDOWMENT FOR THE ARTS IN 1982, THE HIGHEST HONOR THAT THE UNITED STATES BESTOWS ON A FOLK AND A TRADITIONAL ARTIST. HE WAS INDUCTED TO THE S.C. HALL OF FAME IN 1994.

11 | Until The Next Time....

Well, we're back at the Visitor Center after a wonderful historical journey. It's time for goodbyes, answering questions, and giving input on and directions to shopping, eating, sipping, partying and attractions. Some visitors put tips in the slop jar (yay!!), and many share how much that they enjoyed themselves.

Now it's selfie and picture-taking time with various individuals, groups and organizations. In 2008, a Spelman College alumna requested a picture while exiting the bus saying, "Mr. Miller, come and take a picture with *us Spelman Women*." Often, groups request that Mr. Tour Guide take a photo with them and ask permission to post it on Facebook. I can just go to their pages to see the photos. Prior to 2000, folks mailed photos to me. "Time brings on changes!" someone said.

One of my most memorable photo moments was with the jovial Black woman in early 2000 who said, "Oh Honey, take a picture with me." While standing at the side of the bus, she positioned her right arm around Mr. Tour Guide's waist, and Mr. Tour Guide positioned his left arm around her waist. After a big smile, the photo moment was over. Then she said, "Now, my husband is going to kill you." She quickly burst into laughter, and so did Mr. Tour Guide who wondered if she had a husband. I still laugh out loud when thinking about that moment.

Because of the urgency of restroom breaks, some tourists have made a sudden dash off the bus immediately upon arrival back to the Visitor Center: "I need to get to the restroom!" Mr. Buehler exclaimed. "I need to get off now! My husband has the money for the tour and there's a little extra for you," said Mrs. Huntzberry from PA. And there are others who've quietly shared: "I need to be excused." On the other hand, there have been a few instances when the tour ended after the Visitor Center was closed and there were urgent needs for a restroom break. Mr. Tour Guide suggested using the restrooms in the lobby of the nearby Hampton Inn hotel: "Don't ask the desk clerk where the restrooms are because I just told you, you're obviously about to wet on yourself." Once when I mentioned this an older gentleman said, "So in other words Mr. Miller, just go in there and pee!" "Yes sir, just pee," Mr. Tour Guide responded.

Anyway… the next book will cover more of the Charleston peninsula and sections of James and Johns Islands, and of course, I'll relate more of those darndest things that our visitors can say. Until the next time….

Here's *The Charleston Hat Man* For You To Color! He's at 43-47 Broad St. on the Church St. side. This Hat Man replaced a similar one that was painted on the same spot during the late 19th century to advertise the Plenge Haberdashery.

Bibliography

"A Revolutionary Profile: Henry Laurens." South Carolina National Heritage Corridor. Accessed March 10, 2017. http://www.scnhc.org/story/a-revolutionary-profile-henry-laurens.

Battle, Mary, PhD. "Interactive Timeline of Events." A Tribute to the Mother Emanuel Church. May 2016. Accessed January 12, 2017. http://ldhi.library.cofc.edu/exhibits/show/mother-emanuel-tribute/timeline.

Behre, Robert. "Once-endangered home, shop of legendary blacksmith now a museum." Post and Courier. August 15, 2010. Accessed December 10, 2015. http://www.postandcourier.com/columnists/once-endangered-home-shop-of-legendary-blacksmith-now-a-museum/article_885b4f91-f9e7-5020-8cc0-effe1ac48746.html.

Bowers, Paul. "Controversial flag still flying from Spoleto '91." Charleston City Paper. May 30, 2012. Accessed April 22, 2016. http://www.charlestoncitypaper.com/charleston/controversial-flag-still-flying-from-spoleto-91/Content?oid=4085159.

"Broad Street (40-83)." Walled City. Charleston County Public Library - South Carolina. Accessed January 13, 2016. http://www.ccpl.org/content.asp?id=15668&action=detail&catID=6028.

Broughton, Melissa. "Emanuel AME dedicates elevator." *The Post and Courier* (Charleston, SC). June 11, 2016. Accessed December 28, 2016. http://www.postandcourier.com/archives/emanuel-ame-dedicates-elevator/article_4bb94140-e5a4-50a6-916d-851946488e05.html.

"Charles A. Brown High Alumni Association." Accessed March 07, 2017. https://cabhaa.wordpress.com/.

"Charles Towne Landing State Historic Site." South Carolina Parks. Accessed February 03, 2017. http://www.southcarolinaparks.com/ctl/introduction.aspx.

"Charleston's Cigar Factory Strike, 1945-1946." Lowcountry Digital History Initiative. Accessed October 7, 2015. http://ldhi.library.cofc.edu/exhibits/show/cigar_factory/introduction.

"Charleston's Cotton Factory, 1880-1900." Lowcountry Digital History Initiative. Accessed January 3, 2016. http://ldhi.library.cofc.edu/exhibits/show/charlestons-cotton-factory/introduction.

Coffin, Charles Carleton. *The boys of '61, or, Four years of fighting: personal observation with the army and navy, from the first battle of Bull Run to the fall of Richmond*. Boston: Estes and Lauriat, 1885. https://babel.hathitrust.org/cgi/pt?id=uc1.$b41544;view=1up;seq=11.

College of Charleston Advanced GIS Students, et al. *The Charleston Earthquake Tour*. Charleston, SC, nd.

Copp, Roberta VH. "Jones, Jehu." South Carolina Encyclopedia. University of South Carolina, Institute for Southern Studies. June 8, 2016. Accessed January 17, 2017. http://www.scencyclopedia.org/sce/entries/jones-jehu/.

Deakin, Michelle Bates. "Slave Memorial honors builders of Charleston church." UU World Magazine. August 19, 2013. Accessed February 29, 2016. http://www.uuworld.org/articles/slave-memorial-charleston.

"Dock Street Theatre." Charleston, SC - Official Website. Accessed January 16, 2017. http://sc-charleston.civicplus.com/Facilities/Facility/Details/8.

Downs, Kenya. "From Crape Myrtles To Long Houses, Charleston Is A 'Big Barbados'." South Carolina Public Radio. July 21, 2015. Accessed January 19, 2017. http://www.npr.org/2015/07/21/423186974/from-crape-myrtles-to-long-houses-charleston-is-a-big-barbados?utm_campaign=storyshare&utm_source=facebook.com&utm_medium=social&fb_ref=Default.

"Emanuel AME art exhibit and tribute opened to the public." Charleston County Aviation Authority. April 15, 2017. Accessed April 18, 2017. https://www.iflychs.com/News/Emanuel-AME-art-exhibit-and-tribute-opened-to-the.aspx.

Fate, Michael. "Jones, Jehu Jr. (1786-1852)." The Black Past: Remembered and Reclaimed. Accessed January 20, 2017. http://www.blackpast.org/aah/jones-jehu-jr-1786-1852.

Feit, Noah. "Dylann Roof on death row after being transferred to federal custody." thestate.com. April 21, 2017. Accessed April 25, 2017. http://www.thestate.com/news/state/charleston-shootings/article146115349.html.

Fraser, Charles. *Reminiscences of Charleston*. Charleston, SC: J. Russell, 1854. Accessed June 4, 2015. https://catalog.hathitrust.org/Record/007647528.

Frazier, Herb. *'Behind God's Back'*. Charleston, SC: Evening Post Books, 2011.

Frazier, Herb, Bernard Edward Powers, Jr., PhD and Marjory Wentworth. *We are Charleston: Tragedy and Triumph at Mother Emanuel*. Nashville, TN: W Publishing Group, 2016.

Goff, Norvel, Sr., et al. *Morning Grace: Ninety Seconds Changed a Church, Community and the World*. Edited by Herb Frazier. Charleston, SC, 2016.

Gniewekba. "The Friends of the Library Book Club presents 'The Invention Of Wings' at the Blake-Grimké House." College of Charleston Friends of the Library. April 02, 2015. Accessed May 23, 2015. http://friends.library.cofc.edu/?s=grimke.

Gniewekba. "Unveiling of the Grimké Historical Marker." College of Charleston Friends of the Library. February 24, 2015. Accessed May 23, 2015. http://friends.library.cofc.edu/events/event/unveiling-of-the-grimke-historical-marker/.

Greene, Harlan. "Jehu Jones Hotel." Charleston's Free People of Color. Accessed January 11, 2017. http://speccoll.cofc.edu/charlestons-free-people-of-color/jehu-jones-hotel/.

Hatcher, Richard W., III. "H.L. Hunley." South Carolina Encyclopedia. University of South Carolina, Institute for Southern Studies. August 12, 2016. Accessed March 4, 2017. http://www.scencyclopedia.org/sce/entries/h-l-hunley/.

Heffernan, Ashley. "Gibbes Museum of Art Renovation Complete." Charleston Regional Business Journal. May 31, 2016. Accessed February 15, 2017. http://www.charlestonbusiness.com/news/creative-industries/69708/.

Heyward Family Association. Accessed January 25, 2017. http://www.heyward-familyassociation.org/splash-hm-pg/.

Hicks, Brian. "Slavery in Charleston: A chronicle of human bondage in the Holy City." *The Post and Courier* (Charleston, SC). April 09, 2011. Accessed September 8, 2015. http://www.postandcourier.com/news/special_reports/slavery-in-charleston-a-chronicle-of-human-bondage-in-the/article_54334e04-4834-50b7-990b-f81fa3c2804a.html.

Historic Charleston Foundation, comp. and ed. *The City of Charleston Tour Guide Training Manual*. Charleston, SC: City of Charleston, 2011.

Interview in person: Daniel L. Simmons, Jr. on The late Rev. Daniel L. Simmons, Sr., North Charleston, SC. By A.M. Shinault-Small. February 1, 2016.

Interview by telephone: Herb Frazier on The Borough. By A.M. Shinault-Small. January 4, 2017.

Interview in person: Al Miller on Reflections on losing two relatives during the Emanuel AME massacre, North Charleston, SC. By Dr. June Murray. February 19, 2017.

Interview by telephone: Daniel L. Simmons, Jr. on The late Rev. Daniel L. Simmons, Sr., a follow-up. By A.M. Shinault-Small. March 28, 2017.

Jones, Lu Ann, and Robert K. Sutton. *The Life And Legacy Of Robert Smalls of South Carolina's Sea Islands*. Washington, DC: Eastern National, 2012.

Kelly, Jason. "Lorenzo Dow Turner, PhD '26: A linguist who identified the African influences in the Gullah dialect." *University of Chicago Magazine*.

Nov-Dec 2010. Accessed March 15, 2017. http://magazine.uchicago.edu/1012/features/legacy.shtml.

Knich, Diane. "C.A. Brown alums recall school with great fondness." *The Post and Courier*. October 25, 2012. Accessed March 07, 2017. http://www.postandcourier.com/archives/c-a-brown-alums-recall-school-with-great-fondness/article_c0b22c7a-bb0a-57b2-bcaa-4fdcff2576e1.html.

"'Mother Emanuel' A.M.E. Church History." Church History. Accessed December 28, 2016. http://www.emanuelamechurch.org/churchhistory.php.

"Notable Heywards (and Some In-Laws)." Heyward Family Association. Accessed February 1, 2017. http://www.heywardfamilyassociation.org/genealogist-pulpit-2/notable-heywards-and-some-in-laws/.

"Old Slave Mart Museum." Charleston, SC - Official Website. Accessed January 7, 2017. http://sc-charleston.civicplus.com/index.aspx?nid=160.

"Our Story." The Official Site: Gullah Geechee Cultural Heritage Corridor. Accessed September 6, 2016. http://www.gullahgeecheecorridor.org/index.php.

Pearson, Edward A., editor. *Designs against Charleston: The Trial Record of the Denmark Vesey Slave Conspiracy of 1822*. Chapel Hill, NC: University of North Carolina Press, 1999.

"Porgy and Bess, designated as Official Opera of State." South Carolina General Assembly, 114th Session, 2001-2002, Bill 4015. Approved August 29, 2001. Accessed January 25, 2017. http://www.scstatehouse.gov/sess114_2001-2002/bills/4015.htm.

Rosengarten, Dale, et al. *Between The Tracks: Charleston's East Side During The Nineteenth Century*. Charleston, SC: The Charleston Museum and Avery Research Center, 1987.

Shields, David S., PhD. "Evicting the Eagles." charlestonmag.com. December 2015. Accessed November 25, 2016. http://charlestonmag.com/features/evicting_the_eagles.

South Carolina Department of Archives & History. Public Programs Division. *Jehu Jones: Free Black Entrepreneur*. Compiled and authored by Roberta VH Copp. Document Packet No. 1. Columbia, SC: SC Department of Archives & History, 1989.

St. Michael's Church, brochure. *Historical Facts*. Charleston, SC.

Staff, MSRC, "Grimke, Francis" (2015). Manuscript Division. 85. Accessed March 1, 2017. http://dh.howard.edu/finaid_manu/85.

Stello, R. Alan, Jr. *Arsenal of History: the Powder Magazine of South Carolina*. Edited by John R. Young. Charleston, SC: The History Press, 2013.

"Sweet grass basket designated the official handcraft." South Carolina General Assembly, 116th Session, 2005-2006, Bill 3335. Approved February 21, 2006. Accessed May 25, 2015. http://www.scstatehouse.gov/sess116_2005-2006/bills/3335.htm.

The Editors of Encyclopædia Britannica. "Charles F. Richter, American Physicist." Encyclopædia Britannica. January 19, 2010, updated. Accessed September 07, 2016. https://www.britannica.com/biography/Charles-F-Richter.

"The State House History." South Carolina State House. Accessed January 13, 2017. http://www.scstatehouse.gov/studentpage/Explore/history.shtml.

"Visitor Center." Charleston, SC - Official Website. Accessed January 3, 2017. http://sc-charleston.civicplus.com/index.aspx?NID=161.

Waters, Dustin. "Nine life sentences for Roof after he pleads guilty to state charges; grandfather offers apology." charlestoncitypaper.com. April 10, 2017. Accessed April 25, 2017. http://www.charlestoncitypaper.com/TheBattery/archives/2017/04/10/nine-life-sentences-for-roof-after-he-pleads-guilty-to-state-charges.

"Weld-Grimké Family Papers." William L. Clements Library, The University of Michigan. Accessed March 1, 2017. http://quod.lib.umich.edu/c/clementsmss/umich-wcl-M-400wel?view=text.

Weiss, Philip. "Statue of influential Charleston blacksmith Philip Simmons re-dedicated." WCSC, Live 5 News. March 31, 2015. Accessed March 05, 2017. http://www.live5news.com/story/28660544/statue-of-influential-charleston-blacksmith-philip-simmons-rededicated.

Williamson, Joey, et al. "Oleander." Clemson Cooperative Extension. March 2016, revised. Accessed February 6, 2017. http://www.clemson.edu/extension/hgic/plants/landscape/shrubs/hgic1079.html.

Williamson, Samuel H. "Measuring Worth - Relative Value of the US Dollar." Accessed February 3, 2017. https://www.measuringworth.com/uscompare/index.php.

Wise, Warren L. "Relighting interest." Post and Courier. September 4, 2015. Accessed March 6, 2017. http://www.postandcourier.com/business/relighting-interest/article_ab077f28-167d-552a-a531-5c4a25362923.html.

Word, Shout, Song: Lorenzo Dow Turner: Connecting Communities through Language: August 9, 2010-March 27, 2011. Exhibit catalog. Washington D.C.: Anacostia Community Museum, 2010.

Zoppo, Avalon. "Charleston Shooter Dylann Roof Moved to Death Row in Terre Haute Federal Prison." NBCNews.com. April 22, 2017. Accessed April 25, 2017. http://www.nbcnews.com/storyline/charleston-church-shooting/charleston-shooter-dylann-roof-moved-death-row-terre-haute-federal-n749671.

Zuckerman, Catherine. "5 African Foods You Thought Were American." National Geographic. September 21, 2016. Accessed March 13, 2017. http://www.nationalgeographic.com/people-and-culture/food/the-plate/2016/09/5-foods-from-africa/.